THE BESWICK PRICE GUIDE

by
Harvey May

Third edition

Francis Joseph
London
1995

Acknowledgements

Thanks are due to my publisher Francis Salmon for once again encouraging me to revise and update all of the information and prices within these covers and to then put it all together.

Trevor Leak has again been responsible for the cover photograph and many of those contained in the book. I must also thank Marilyn and Peter Sweet, Chris Lane (Australia) Lyndsey and Jim Otter and Glynis for their help in either providing photographs or pieces to be photographed.

My daughter-in-law, Lesley, has done much of the typing and my wife Hazel has been a constant help throughout and her support is so necessary in a project of this kind. Thank you both.

Mary Moorcroft, Public Relations Executive at Royal Doulton, has again been helpful in providing photographs of new products.

I would also like to thank the large numbers of collectors and dealers who are always willing to share informaton with me and to advise model variations and unusual colourways which they have found.

Harvey May

Important Notice

All the information contained in this book has been compiled from reliable sources and every effort has been made to eliminate errors. Neither the publishers nor the author can be held responsible for losses which may occur in the purchase, sale or other transaction of items because of the information contained herein. Readers who feel they have discovered errors are invited to write and inform us so that these may be corrected in subsequent editions.

Royal Doulton plc is in no way associated with this publication, which is produced independently.

Third Edition
Francis Joseph Publishing
All rights reserved. No unauthorised publication or photocopying of information contained in this publication is permitted.

©1995 Harvey May and Francis Joseph Publishing.
Beswick is a registered trademark of Royal Doulton Ltd.

Typeset by E J Folkard Print Services
199 Station Road, Crayford, Kent DA1 3QF

Printed by The Greenwich Press
Standard House, Westmoor Street, London SE7.

To my sons
Andrew and Jeffrey
who have for the past ten years
had to put up with their
father's pet hobby —
collecting Beswick

About the Author

Harvey May was born in Wood Green, London in 1932, the son of a Durham miner who had moved to London after the General Strike of 1926. During the war years he was a child evacuee moving from London to the country town of Halstead, Essex. After the interruption of the war years Harvey finished his education at Enfield Technical School and left there to start work in 1949. He married Hazel in 1954 and moved to his present home in Essex in 1958. He has two sons, both married, and three grandsons, who each have their own growing collection.

His first interest in any hobby was the modest but popular schoolboy pastime of collecting bus and train numbers, an interest which took him far and wide on similarly modest transport — his bike!

In 1952 Harvey joined British Railways as Technical Assistant in the Civil Engineer's Office at King's Cross station, but has now retired from the railway. Throughout this time he has amassed a collection of railway items and many related books.

China and crested ware have always been an area of interest for Harvey and it was the chance purchase of a Beswick Penguin in 1980 which led to a large collection and the quest for information.

The results of his efforts lie between the covers of this book, to be enjoyed by equally enthusiastic collectors.

Contents

Introduction   7

Collecting Beswick   11

A Century of Progress!   15

Part One: ANIMALS

Birds   22

Bird Wall Plaques   26

Butterfly Plaques   26

Cats   27

Connoisseur Series   28

Colin Melbourne Models   30

Dogs   31

Farm Animals   35

Fish   37

Horses, mounted horses, heavy horses, ponies and wall plaques   38

Wild Animals   46

Part Two: CHARACTER WARES

Character and Toby Jugs, Teapots and Derivatives   81

Characters from Film and Literature: 84
  (Listed in the following catagories: Beatrix Potter, Snow White
  and the 7 Dwarfs, Winnie the Pooh, Alice in Wonderland,
  Kitty Macbride, Walt Disney, Rupert Bear, Wind in the Willows,
  Thelwell Figures, David Hand Animal Figures)

Comical Animals and Birds   94

English Country Folk   97

Pig Prom — Musicians   97

Figures   98

Little Loveables   100

Thunderbirds   102

Little Likeables   102

Studio Sculptures   104

Beswick Bears   105

Country Cousins   106

Wall Plaques and Masks   106

Part Three: DECORATIVE WARES

Advertising Ware   109

Christmas Around the World (Plates)   112

Christmas Carol Tankards   113

Commemoratives   114

Shakespeare Series Ware   115

Trentham Art Wares   116

Britannia Collection   117

Catalogue Specials   118

Models mounted on a wood plinth   118

BACKSTAMPS   119

Introduction

From the Author

Welcome to this third edition of the *Beswick Price Guide*.

In the two years since my last edition appeared, there have been some significant events in the world of Beswick. Probably the most important was the appearance of a number of new models, each carrying the Beswick backstamp.

This has given a boost to collectors and a general feeling that the backstamp is here to stay, at least for the foreseeable future. It surely must be easier to build on the past success of a trade mark than to diminish its availability and replace it with another.

1993 saw the first ever large size Beatrix Potter model and the one chosen was Peter Rabbit. There have subsequently been seven further characters, modelled to the same large size, but only one other carries the Beswick mark.

The real surprise introduction and a 'first' for Beswick, was the set of six busts, based upon characters from the TV series *Thunderbirds* and only available by post in a numbered edition of 2,500. Other new introductions, within two years, amounted to some 80 models and this formidable list includes the six superb *Pig's Prom*, the eight very detailed *Country Friends*, three Badgers, a Harvest Mouse and a Wood Mouse, ten small size Dogs and several farm animals from the current range, now available on bases. The 16 remaining original medium size dogs have now been withdrawn.

To mark Beswick's Centenary in 1994, the special size 'Jemima Puddleduck' figure is accompanied by 'Cancara', the black horse, both carrying the Beswick stamp for 1994 only. These models herald a new era in the development of the Beswick brand and are most welcome additions to the range.

Overall, I think Beswick collectors have been given a great deal of consideration, and it is to be hoped that Royal Doulton will have one or two more surprises in store. This may be a good time to state, quite categorically, that the John Beswick factory is still very much in business and has a very full production schedule. All 130 Beswick-marked models still in production are made and decorated here, along with a wide range of Royal Doulton marked character jugs and figures and, of course, all of the Beatrix Potter models, marked Royal Albert, are made here also.

It is surprising how many people believe that the Beswick factory is closed. In fact, there is a fine museum with a good representative collection of many of the older decorative wares and figures, together with a showroom containing current production pieces. Factory tours are available, Monday-Friday, both morning and afternoon, and are thoroughly recommended. The tour takes about 1¼ hours and finishes in the factory shop, where there is a good range of products for sale, frequently at advantageous prices.

The factory is in Gold Street, Longton, Stoke-on-Trent and tours can be arranged through Joan Barker, telephone 01782 291213 or Royal Doulton on 01782 292292. The Gladstone Pottery Museum is nearby and the two can be conveniently visited in one day.

Since my last book was published, Beswick models have continued to increase in popularity and some of the well liked items are now very hard to find. Even the more common pieces are sometimes quite difficult to find and, of course, the rarer models command a much higher price.

Details of all models which have been allocated a shape number in the Beswick pattern book are again listed under the different headings and are up-to-date with regard to new introductions and withdrawals.

Throughout the book, a model which is still made today at the Beswick factory is marked 'C' in the lists. The price quoted is the Current Suggested Retail Selling Price, including 17½% VAT, as given in the January 1995 price list published by Royal Doulton.

Top favourites still seem to be the Beatrix Potter models, although the several Walt Disney and David hand series are very much in demand.

Marilyn Sweet's *Guide to Horses, Ponies & Foals* published in 1992, filled the gap very nicely and was well received by all collectors of horses.

All models in the following groups, and which originally carried the Beswick mark, are now in the Royal Doulton series and a new DA (Doulton Animals) number has been allocated:

1) Connoisseur
2) Horses
3) Foals
4) 'Fireside' Dogs and Cat
5) Old English Dogs (1378/3 to 1378/7)
6) Dogs (medium) 3055 and above
7) Spirit Dogs on plinth (matt)
8) 'Good Companion' Dogs (2982 and above)
9) Cats

All now carry the Royal Doulton backstamp, and all are still made in the Beswick factory. Full details of the new DA and old Beswick numbers are given and will help identification.

Now that the initial upset amongst collectors over the use of the Royal Albert mark on Beatrix Potter figures has died down, it is time to see what effect it has had.

First of all, there has been a very long 'offer' period on the standard price figures, with 1993 seeing the price at £9.95 and the 1994 price being £10.95. Both years saw these prices held for varying periods and sales should have been quite healthy. December 1993 also saw the withdrawal of no fewer than twelve figures, of which one (2971) had never carried the Beswick mark and two (3031 and 3091) had only carried the Beswick mark for about 18 months before changing to Royal Albert in August 1989. December 1994 saw the withdrawal of six more figures, of which three (3030, 3090 and 3094) had again only carried the Beswick mark for about two years before changing to Royal Albert, and the other three (3197, 3252 and 3257) had only carried the Royal Albert mark.

Advance notice has been given that six more are to be withdrawn at the end of 1995. Four (1106, 1676, 2509 and 2956) are original Beswick models and the other two (3157 and 3251) are Royal Albert only.

So we now have a situation where Royal Doulton themselves are creating a collectors' market by the early withdrawal of figures from a very popular range. New model variations continue to turn up and this adds a bit of spice for the observant collector. No records were kept of these changes as they were mostly made to ease production problems.

Three other new and largely unannounced series, totalling 63 models, have appeared during the past two years, with varying degrees of success. The first group was a set of seven different clown models, all under the series name of *Little Loveables*, and each had a printed message on the top of the base (e.g. 'To Mother'). Each was available in three different colourways, two in gloss finish and one in matt and so 21 models were initially available, with the matt finish being much harder to find.

Within a few months of being launched, the model with the logo 'God Loves Me' was replaced with 'Please'. This straightaway made a rarity and almost immediately the seven models also became available with no logo at all — but only in gloss! This made 28 different models altogether and, more recently, there have been six new additions. All have now been withdrawn.

Members of the Beswick Collectors Circle will be able to purchase a special logo model marked 'I Love Beswick' and this will make a series total of 35.

The second group suddenly appeared at only a handful of outlets and without any publicity at all towards the end of 1993. They were resin models of bears, about 3" high and all doing something different and enjoying a picnic party. Superbly detailed and carrying a *Beswick Bears* label on the base, each piece was named and carried a suitable verse (e.g. 'Sam' plays his banjo all day long, amusing friends with a tune and a song). Standard green Beswick boxes were used for packaging, with *Beswick Bears* printed on the side.

Very limited marketing appears to have taken place and the whole series has now largely disappeared from retail outlets. The oft heard comment that 'collectors are not aware of new products' certainly seems to be true in the case of the Bears and, to a lesser extent, the *Little Loveables*.

The third group appeared in October 1994, were again of resin and very similar to the Bears. The series was named *Country Cousins* and portrayed several different small animals. They are numbered PM2101 to PM2120 but only 17 models seem to be available at present. They are marketed with a brand name of 'Beswick International' and made in (the country of) China.

There has again been an increased awareness of collecting Beswick in Australia, New Zealand, South Africa, North America and Canada and membership of the Beswick Collectors Circle is now about 750.

Many new collectors of Beswick have already been interested in Doulton for a number of years and are merely broadening their horizons, but there are also a very sizeable number of new collectors who have been attracted to Beswick.

All of this activity points to a healthy collecting market and it is hoped that new models will continue to attract the attention of collectors. Values have continued to rise in some collecting areas and there have been some pretty spectacular prices paid at some of the specialist auctions. There have also been some price reductions, as collecting habits have changed and ideas modified. There are now four major UK collectors fairs which feature Beswick alongside the well-established Doulton wares. These are held at Stafford, in early May, at Dunstable in October, and the newest fair, organised by the Doulton and Beswick Dealers Association, is held at the Birmingham Motor Cycle Museum in March and August.

A frequent request since Beswick became so popular was for more pictures and this was met, during 1994, with the publication by UK International Ceramics of a special numbered limited edition of 1,000 copies of a 1959 Beswick catalogue. With over 600 illustrations, it nicely fills the pictorial gap for collectors.

Some items which have been listed in the three previous Beswick collectors books have been taken out of this edition and will appear in the more suitable *Decorative Wares Handbook* which is in the course of preparation.

This leads me to remind you that all prices quoted are only a guide as to what you might expect to pay. They are not auction results but average Fair prices and you must **always** make your **own** decision on what you actually pay, depending on condition.

Collecting Beswick

My interest developed from collecting crested china wares which are, on the whole, not very colourful. Visiting antique fairs is an enjoyable way of not only looking for something which is pleasing to the eye, but also where you can meet people and, quite often, make friends. Everyone acquires knowledge about their hobby and it is only by sharing information that we all learn more.

It was in the early 1980s that, whilst visiting a Fair, a penguin with an orange umbrella over its head caught my eye. The modelling and touch of humour appealed to me and my first purchase of Beswick took place at the modest price of £2!

The seeds of collecting were sown and I was hooked!

Gradually I built up a small collection of pieces and regularly attended Fairs simply to look for more Beswick. Questions arose — 'How many are there in the set?' 'Who modelled this or that piece?' 'When was it made?'

There were few answers forthcoming from dealers, who only put Beswick on their shelves because of its obvious quality.

So began my quest for more knowledge and also research to find some answers to the many questions which I had, not least of which was 'Who are Beswick?', 'When did they start?', 'What makes them produce the things they do?'

The more I researched through old catalogues the more I became aware of the great diversity and range of Beswick, from colourful Christmas tankards to the spectacular lifelike models of wild animals, such as the African Elephant. The company has consistently produced excellent models of horses, dogs and wild animals, and is well established as a specialist in its field.

Many of the Beswick models are superb and I think that the Connoisseur Collection, in particular, represents the very best in artistic design and detail. The subjects cover award-winning show dogs, famous racehorses, wild animals and birds, all on a mahogany plinth and ready to take pride of place on any collector's shelf.

Beswick models are not only accurate and detailed but are appealing to! Humour is very much to the fore, as in the cat playing the violin or the happy mongrel dog with outrageously proportioned limbs and head. Even models not specifically intended to be funny are often engaging in their poses, and this certainly adds to the enjoyment of collecting.

The Company has certainly stood the test of time and the basis of this success can be attributed mainly to the work of John Ewart and Gilbert Beswick who broke new ground in the thirties.

Art Director James Hayward also deserves special mention here because he had over thirty designers working under him during the period 1934 to 1969 when Royal Doulton took over the company and he continued to work for Beswick until his retirement in 1975.

The number of people who are Beswick collectors is very considerable and, through them, I am able to keep 'tabs' on most of the model variations which turn up.

My initial research into Beswick history and product information was hampered by the very limited amount available and so I contacted the factory for help. Very little was available and I was invited to examine the old pottery books. From these and other sources I have been able to trace the production details of Beswick's output since the 1930s.

With more knowledge gained during the last ten years, I have updated all of the lists with the latest available information on variations, colours and prices and I hope that you will be able to 'pin down' those unusual finds. Additionally, I have noted models finished in a matt deco, together with their production run.

I am still being advised of Beswick 'lookalikes', which appear to be genuine but are not. The latest is a rather crude attempt at stamping Beswick England on the belly of farm and wild animals from another factory. Another advice was of 'Beswick England' being hand lettered on the belly of dogs. The latest is an attempt at producing B.P. figures with 'Gold' backstamps. None of these should fool the genuine collector.

Once again, I hope that you will enjoy this book which, if not your introduction to the world of Beswick, will at least update your knowledge a little.

Collecting Tips
and Valuing Discontinued Beswick

Once collectors become 'hooked' they often find it difficult to know when to stop buying and this can create all kinds of problems, particularly if the pieces are very expensive. Beswick wares are now very collectable and some prices have risen steeply during the last two years. No longer is it possible to find relatively rare models at bargain prices. The number of possible collecting subjects is enormous though and the best way of starting is by choosing a specific theme such as 'Horses', 'Beatrix Potters' or 'humorous subjects'.

This book gives details of the variety available, but it is a good idea to find out what the current price range is for the chosen pieces before embarking on an area which is too expensive. It is no good deciding to collect a particular series without knowing how many pieces there are and how much you are likely to have to spend to make a complete collection.

The only guide as to the value or worth of a particular piece is the amount that the collector is prepared to spend. As the market for Beswick continues to develop, collectors will become more and more aware of which models are the hardest to find and, in accordance with the dictates of supply and demand, the prices of these are bound to rise more than the rest. This is what makes collecting so enjoyable, particularly the pleasure of a 'find' which is picked up at a reasonable price.

The collector will find this book useful for identifying models, their dates of production and withdrawal, but it must be noted that some of the pieces do not have the model number impressed on their base and that where the base is too small for the Beswick mark it may only have the 'England' stamp on it. In these cases the collector, coming across the model for the first time at an antiques fair, may not recognise it as Beswick.

PLEASE NOTE THAT MODELS PREVIOUSLY AVAILABLE WITH A BESWICK BACKSTAMP, BUT NOW CURRENTLY AVAILABLE WITH EITHER A ROYAL DOULTON OR ROYAL ALBERT MARK, COMMAND A HIGHER PRICE AS DISCONTINUED BESWICK.

The difficulties involved in finding the final additions to a collection add to the pleasure of 'the hunt', which is, after all, what it is all about. GOOD HUNTING!

*Introduced in 1983 as part of the Connoisseur Series; **2725** Cheetah on Rock*

Model Numbers

So far as is known every item produced since 1933 has been allocated a model number.

In some cases, for example wall mounted plaques of birds in flight, sets of different size models will be given the same number.

Colour variations also occur among animals, Dickens ware and B.P. figures, with the same number applying each time. Many of the animals are available in either gloss or matt finish and some can be found with or without a china or wooden base. In all cases the same model number applies.

Most of the pre-war bird, wild and farm animal models were decorated in several different colours. The more unusual shades command a higher price. A popular was blue – usually marked 8700 – and this was used on many early models and in all groups.

Dates of withdrawal are given with information taken from annual price lists.

The following table gives the design date for each model:

Model Numbers			Design Date	Model Numbers			Design Date
1	—	377	Undated	1921	—	1996	1964
378	—	460	1936	1997	—	2053	1965
461	—	567	1937	2054	—	2086	1966
568	—	672	1938	2087	—	2176	1967
673	—	794	1939	2177	—	2255	1968
795	—	880	1940	2256	—	2302	1969
881	—	968	1941	2303	—	2349	1970
969	—	990	1942	2350	—	2396	1971
991	—	1000	1943	2397	—	2443	1972
1001	—	1013	1944	2444	—	2500	1973
1014	—	1042	1945	2501	—	2522	1974
1043	—	1082	1946	2523	—	2554	1975
1083	—	1107	1947	2555	—	2582	1976
1108	—	1141	1948	2583	—	2607	1977
1142	—	1180	1949	2608	—	2636	1978
1181	—	1209	1950	2637	—	2666	1979
1210	—	1226	1951	2667	—	2700	1980
1227	—	1279	1952	2701	—	2750	1981
1280	—	1322	1953	2751	—	2804	1982
1323	—	1362	1954	2805	—	2846	1983
1363	—	1391	1955	2847	—	2899	1984
1392	—	1468	1956	2900	—	2960	1985
1469	—	1516	1957	2961	—	3031	1986
1517	—	1576	1958	3032	—	3114	1987
1577	—	1667	1959	3115	—	3179	1988
1668	—	1732	1960	3180	—	3225	1989
1733	—	1792	1961	3226	—	3275	1990
1793	—	1861	1962	3276	—	3330	1991
1862	—	1920	1963	3331	—		1992

A Century of Progress!

How proud James Wright Beswick would have been to know that the family potting business, started in 1894, would be celebrating its centenary this year and still producing high quality products under the umbrella of Royal Doulton (UK) Limited.

The Beswicks were originally from Bolton, in Lancashire – the cotton county – and during the 1830s they moved to the parish of Chell, in Staffordshire, where they soon developed coal interests.

In 1840, Robert Beswick, in partnership with John Leese, bought a piece of land in Tunstall and built a small 'pot bank'. There were already hundreds of similar small factories producing earthenware and rough-cast figures and competition must have been fierce. The factory was named 'Churchbank' and manufacture of earthenwares commenced straight away and continued until 1857 when it was leased out, with a condition that 'all coal for potting should be supplied from Beswick-owned mines'. No significant change took place until 1891 when 'Churchbank' was sold to Thomas Booth, who developed 'good quality earthenware shapes, delicately potted and light in weight'.

Meanwhile, the coal mine was being run by Robert Beswick's two sons, Robert and James Wright, and it was the latter who, in 1894, went into business on his own and established a potting trade in Longton, one of the six towns which make up the Staffordshire Potteries.

He took a five-year lease on the Baltimore Works in Albion Street and production of an increasing variety of plain and decorated ware commenced.

Two years later, the lease of a second factory – the Britannia Works in Longton High Street – was taken and then again, in 1898, a third lease, this time to the present home of Beswick, the Gold Street Works.

Expansion here was fast and additional kilns were quickly built and contributed to a 'very modern and completely fitted-up factory'.

The following year – 1899 – saw the Baltimore Works lease run out and all china production appears to have been concentrated at the Brittania Works. Everything points to the production of china having been ceased here when the lease ran out in 1905.

Meanwhile, expansion at Gold Street continued and James Wright's eldest son, John, who had been involved in the business for a number of years, was made a partner with a salary of £4 per week and he immediately took control of manufacturing.

According to a report in the March 1906 *Pottery Gazette* '. . . almost everything in earthenware is made here . . .' and special mention is made of chimney ornaments.

It is of interest here to say that Royal Doulton currently produce five Traditional Staffordshire Dog models still using the original Beswick moulds.

In 1908, the works of Bridgett & Bates in King Street, Longton were acquired, so that china production could re-establish once again.

Production of china marked 'Aldwych China' continued here until 1914 when the factory was closed down, sold and production transferred to the more modern Warwick Works in Chadwick Street, Longton. The factory was probably leased until being taken over in 1918 and all china produced here, from that time, was backstamped 'Beswick & Sons'.

Earthenware production continued at the Gold Street Works, whilst all china was made at Chadwick Street until this factory closed in the early 1930s.

The company had now enjoyed 20 years of uninterrupted expansion and had survived the Great War. Their products were aimed at the popular market and prices were consistently below those of their rivals. New introductions kept the interests of retailers and consumers and there was a constant improvement in quality. Trade was brisk and Beswick began exporting to the Dominions.

By 1919, consumers were again buying the things which had been denied them during the war and the trade boom quickly helped to re-establish the pottery trade once again.

In May, 1920 at the age of 75, James Wright Beswick died and the firm was taken over by his son, John. James Wright Beswick had never been properly trained as a potter and he had learnt by trial and error and common sense. His son, John, had the advantage of some technical training and had also attended classes at the Pottery School in Tunstall.

James Wright Beswick was a JP, a member of the old Longton Council, member of Kidsgrove on the first Staffordshire County Council and, later, a Councillor for the City of Stoke-on-Trent. He was also a prominent leader in the Methodist Church affairs and chairman of the old Longton School Board.

The potting trade now suffered the effects of the depression and there was very limited opportunity to make any significant improvement. John Beswick was now the Managing Director at the age of 51 and he was to steer the company through the twenties and into the thirties with a careful policy of improving quality and concentrating more on ornamental ware production.

Beswick products at this time consisted of toiletware, gilt and enamelled jugs and vases, decorated dishes and fruit bowls, together with many other decorative shapes. China and tea ware from the Warwick Works was of fine quality and used the decorative technique of tint-on-print (colouring in parts of transfer prints) on many items. Gilding was still carried out and did not stop until the mid-sixties.

The Beswick family tree is complex and Gilbert (John's stepbrother) went to work at Beswick, after leaving High School in about 1922, and seems to have spent much of his time in the decorating shop. This was to have far-reaching effects later on and was also a contributing factor in Beswick's success story.

In 1926 two men, who were to become central figures in the team, joined the company – Jim Hayward, the future Art Director and Albert Hallam, who was to become acknowledged as the most talented mould-maker in the Potteries.

Like most people living in the Potteries, Jim Hayward came from a family which, for many generations, had been involved in the pottery industry at Coalport in Coalbrookdale. His career began at the Royal Art Factory, Longton where he was apprenticed to his father. At 16 he left as a protest against working with lead paint without protection and joined Beswick as a painter improver. He was appointed Assistant Manager to Mr Dean, the Decorating Manager, and when Mr Dean departed in 1934 he became Decorating Manager.

Albert Hallam joined Beswick in 1926 at the age of fourteen as an apprentice mould-maker. His father, also called Albert, was already a Beswick clay manager and it was not long before young Albert became a 'block and caser' and eventually head of the mould-making department. Following further training, he became a modeller and was better able to understand the problems of making moulds.

By 1933, Jim Hayward, together with Mr. Dean, had perfected a range of new matt glazes with which they decorated a variety of ornamental ware, all colour being applied with a spray. A piece of sponge was used if a stippled effected was wanted.

Ultimately, more than 50 girls were employed to meet the demand and the Beswick 'Matt Glaze Girls' became famous throughout the potteries.

John Beswick died in 1934 and his son John Ewart became Chairman and Managing Director.

There was now a team in place which was to remain together until the mid-1970s. The only addition would be in 1939 when Arthur Gredington joined the company as its first resident sculptor. Up until this time, much work had been by freelance modellers and certainly nothing like Arthur Gredington's very first model had been seen before at Beswick.

Racehorse 'Bois Russel' won the 1939 Derby and was entered in the Beswick pattern book in March 1939 as model no 701. It was the first realistically modelled horse by Beswick and the forerunner of more than 70 different horse models by Arthur Gredington, up until his final one in 1968.

Gilbert Beswick was now the Sales Director and his 'shop-floor' knowledge was to prove invaluable in being able to accept orders, often with tight delivery times, and to assess likely production problems which might arise. He was a kindly man, a lifelong member of the local Bourne Methodist Church, loved and respected by both employees and customers, but unfortunately the best interests of the Company were not always given priority.

He would agree to very small orders from agents, specially decorated horses and dogs for customers (with detail taken from photographs) and for special items to be modelled, with limited appeal to the market as a whole.

Many of these orders made little or no profit for the factory and caused friction with Ewart Beswick. This led to disagreements, which affected everyone and he would not admit to having made wrong decisions. Later, he would realise his mistakes and apologise and express regret for the upset caused.

Despite this, he was greatly concerned with employee's family troubles and welfare and gave much practical help and kindness, when necessary. Many of the factory workers were members of the Bourne Church and many followed their parents in obtaining employment at Beswicks.

When children reached the age of 14 and had attended Chapel and Sunday School regularly and whose parents were already employed at Beswicks, then Gilbert would say to them 'when you leave school, you come and see me'. When the time came, the child would speak to Gilbert and be told to 'come along to Beswick on Monday at 7am.' Being the youngest meant doing all sorts of jobs and stoking up the fires was one which was important, so that at 9.30am, when there was a breakfast break, you could have a hot drink and cook bacon and egg, if you had taken it with you. The next job was brushing up all the fires and generally tidying up. There were no canteen facilities, unlike today, and you had to stand in a queue to make tea. If you had a meat pie with for dinner, this could be heated on the fire, together with potatoes and vegetables, which would be cooked in a chamber pot.

Other odd jobs would be carried out around the factory and gradually the child would see the different processes being carried out. Everyone would go home at 5.30pm except the two youngest employees and they would stay until 6pm and do all the sweeping up, before taking the post to the post box.

Saturday mornings were worked from 7am to 12.30pm and one week's paid holiday was given. If you did not go away, you could work as usual.

Youngsters often started learning on the white (undecorated) ware and collected finished pieces for packing. Then, when extra help was needed, they were given some of the less coloured ware to decorate; chambers, ewers, posy bowls and jugs, but not dinner plates.

When Gilbert thought that you knew what you were going, he would allow you to try something else. He would be all over the factory, every day,

Ewart Beswick   *Gilbert Beswick*

and he would himself start at 8am and would first of all check that all staff were in.

Quality was the first priority and if work was not up to standard, then Gilbert would soon tell the person responsible. Jim Hayward, Decorating Manager, would often stand at the door of the decorating shop and watch the girls decorating the ware and if they did not do it right, he would show them the correct way.

The number of employees at Beswick in the late 1930s was around 100 and fifty years later this had risen to around 500. There are currently approximately 380 employed at Beswick.

In 1938 the business became a private limited company (John Beswick Ltd) and was converted to a public company in 1957.

Decorators usually stayed on the same type of work, some did cottage ware and others salad ware and there was no painting on tea ware. One person would usually stick to the same pattern and this explains why there is frequently very little to choose between several of the earlier decorative pieces when some of the same pattern are compared.

Tube lining and gilding were all carried out by one person until work of this nature ceased in the mid-1960s. All decorating colours were individual and had to be mixed up as required. Aerographers were each given half a pint of milk daily and this was usually boiled up and used as a hot drink. The rate of pay for a girl decorator, at the age of 21, was £1.15 per 5½ day week. Aerographing uses a quick drying water-based paint which is sprayed on and dries as a powder. Using a clean dry brush, any desired decorative effect can be obtained by brushing off some of the paint. This process is used on both vases and animal figures.

Firing of the ware meant that the man in charge of the bottle oven was responsible for the most critical part of the whole process of pottery production. He was the highest paid employee and was in charge of the whole output from the factory covering several days. Bad firing could result in severe losses and he would have to stay up with each oven, for probably 60 hours or more, to ensure that all was well. Ventilation had to be adjusted and temperature maintained and probably 10 tonnes of coal would have to be shovelled – by hand. Is it any wonder that vast quantities of ale were consumed!

When the wares in the bottle oven were ready and it was judged possible to enter, the men went in wearing only a cap and an old sack or piece of cloth tied around their middle and frequently no shoes! Sweat would pour off them as they climbed inside and right up to the top to get the wares out. This was generally about 16 feet up and wooden ladders called 'osses' were used. The wares were in clay containers called 'saggars' and they each weighed about 40-50lbs. An oven might contain up to 2,000 saggars.

When the oven had been cleared each man would be paid 12½p 'beer money' and his services would no longer be required.

The ovens were drawn once a week and every other week a smaller oven was drawn. On these days there would be a queue outside Beswick and if there were insufficient regular workers, then the wares man would go down

Arthur Gredington, modeller from 1939 to 1968.

Albert Hallam, mould maker and modeller from 1926-75.

and make a selection. If you were a good worker, then you would be asked to come again. There was no need to employ the men full time.

During the 1939-45 war a large amount of plain white earthenware was supplied to the RAF but all other items continued in production on a much-reduced scale. Beswick had bought the adjoining China Bank of H. M. Williamson (trading as Heathcote China) in 1941 and it is here that the RAF earthenware was made.

With the ending of the war, there was no sudden return to normality. Shortages of raw materials, transport difficulties and Government restrictions on both production and decorated ware meant that much development was stifled.

The early 1950s saw the same management team at the helm and plans for expansion were made. In 1957 the adjoining firm of Thomas Lawrence (trading as Falcon Ware) was bought and considerable alterations and rebuilding took place and a lot of the old Beswick buildings were knocked down.

It is believed that the bottle ovens were demolished when rebuilding took place and these were replaced by modern gas-fired tunnel ovens where the gradually rising and strictly controlled temperatures reaches a maximum of 1170°C.

In 1961 Harry Sales left E. Brain & Co. and started work at Beswick as a Modelling Assistant to Jim Hayward, the Art Director. When Jim Hayward retired in 1975, Harry Sales was appointed Design Manager, a position he held until 1986.

Graham Tongue joined Beswick in April 1966 and became head modeller when Albert Hallam retired in 1973. When Harry Sales left in 1986 Graham took over responsibility for both design and modelling. Two other modellers worked for Beswick, David Lyttleton from 1973-86 and Alan Maslankowski from 1973-76. Both still model occasionally for Beswick.

By the late 1960s Ewart Beswick was ready to retire and had no son or heir to whom he could pass control of his business. The Company's reputation was such that it was bought by Royal Doulton, as part of its own development plants, in 1969.

At this time, in addition to the animal, bird and figure ranges, there were still over 100 different ornamental items in production, together with modern designs in the 'Kashan' vase range and 'Zorba' and 'Orbit' tableware.

By the end of 1973 all tableware and vase production had ceased and there was naturally an increasing Royal Doulton influence on design.

The Bunnikins series commenced in 1972 and the design and production has continued there ever since, alongside Brambly Hedge, Winnie the Pooh and Beatrix Potter figures.

The Beswick factory is a friendly place in which to work and with a varying range of figures, character jugs, horses, birds and animals being produced, the future looks secure.

The popular 'Beswick England' backstamp is still used on many of the products coming from the factory and these stand proudly alongside others carrying the Royal Doulton or Royal Albert mark.

Marketing of the John Beswick brand name has recently been enhanced by the introduction of the nine 'Little Loveable' clown models, the five 'Country Figures', the limited edition set of six 'Thunderbird' characters and the large size model of Peter Rabbit.

These fine new additions are a tribute to Beswick's continuing expertise in this area of ceramics.

Today, Graham Tongue has a modelling team consisting of Warren Platt and Martyn Alcock, who both joined the John Beswick Studio at Gold Street in 1986 along with Amanda Hughes-Lubeck who joined in 1988.

Gordon Lawton with Jim Hayward (right) with the author at back at a Beswick Open Day in 1987.

Part One: Animals

The name of Beswick is synonymous with meticulously faithful models of animals. The appointment of Arthur Gredington as modeller in 1939 was a major factor in the success of Beswick, for his original models were outstanding. When his skill was combined with that of mouldmaker, Arthur Hallam, and the patient attention and detail of the Beswick paintresses, the quality of the finished Beswick animal was assured.

Birds

(All current birds carry a Beswick backstamp)

Many varieties and styles of birds are to be found in the Beswick collection. The earliest models were of a ornamental nature, but they soon became more realistic. Later on in the 1930s it became fashionable to model birds in the form of wall plaques and today these are a very collectable series. Mr Watkin was the chief exponent of these particular ornaments and he followed his success with ducks by introducing sets of seagulls, pheasants and blue-tits in flight.

In contrast to the birds on the wing, Beswick artists also modelled a number of species of birds perched on boughs and tree trunks adorned with flowers and these were particularly popular in the late thirties. Until around 1965 the petals and leaves on the bases were modelled in high relief, but as these were vulnerable to damage they were subsequently replaced with hand-painted flowers in low relief.

During the 1950s Colin Melbourne modelled some birds in the modern style, and these were known and marked as the 'C.M.' series and numbered in the '1400' range. He was also responsible for the collection of decoy ducks (1518-1529) which were modelled from the birds sheltering in Peter Scott's sanctuary at Slimbridge. Jim Hayward was the Art Director at the time and he visited Peter Scott to select the species to be portrayed. The first model in this set of twelve was produced in four sizes (see listing), the next two in three sizes and the remaining birds were made in one size only. These models are very collectable, and hard to find.

In recent years Graham Tongue has tended to work on the bird collection. To ensure that his models are accurate, he visits local aviaries and also the Natural History department of the City Museum and Art Gallery, Stoke-on-Trent, and the results of his research are evident in his studies for the Connoisseur range, the Golden Eagle (2062) and the Pheasant (2760). Since 1983 models have been available in either glossy or matt finish, with the exception of the Pheasant (2760).

More recently he has sculpted some superb pieces, but these all now carry the Royal Doulton backstamp and therefore are not be listed here.

Two of the small size birds, introduced in 1991, were modelled by Martyn Alcock, who joined Beswick in 1986 on a Youth Training Scheme. He has since modelled a wide variety of pieces, under Graham's watchful eye.

With regard to the eight small birds, each in two versions, the best way to tell the difference is to look for the impressed number and 'B' backstamp on the base. These only appy to the first versions.

Model No	Name of Model	Size inches	Current Value £	$	Production Period
450/1	Penguin	8	75-85	150-180	1936-1940
450/2	Penguin	3½	40-45	80-90	1936-1955
617	Duck	3	40-45	80-95	1938-1955
618	Puffin	—	55-65	110-140	1938-1955
749	Mallard (rising)	6½	85-100	180-200	1939-1965
750	Mallard (settling)	6½	85-100	180-200	1939-1965
754	Pheasant ash tray	3½	10-15	20-30	1939-1971
755	Duck ash tray	4	10-15	20-30	1939-1969
756/1	Mallard	7	35-40	70-80	1939-1973
756/2	Mallard	5¾	25-30	50-60	1939-1973
756/2A	Mallard	4½	20-25	40-55	1939-1973
756/3	Mallard	3½	15-20	30-40	1939-1973
767	Pheasant (curved tail)	3	10-15	20-30	1939-1971
*767	Pheasant (straight tail)	3	5-10	15-20	1971-1994
768	Seagull	8½	125-150	250-350	1939-1955
800	Penguin (Small)	2	10-15	20-30	1940-1973
801	Penguin (Small)	2	10-15	20-30	1940-1973
	Part of set (see 802 & 803 Novelties)				
817/1	Mallard	7½	90-105	190-215	1940-1969
817/2	Mallard	6¾	80-90	175-200	1940-1969
820	Pair of Geese	4	20-25	40-50	1940-1973
821	Gosling	2¼	10-15	20-30	1940-1973
822	Gosling	1¾	10-15	20-30	1940-1973
827/1	Goose	7½	60-70	130-150	1940-1955
827/2	Goose	6	55-65	110-130	1940-1955
827/3	Goose	5	50-60	100-120	1940-1955
849	Pheasant (in flight) Wings up	6	85-100	175-200	1940-1971
850	Pheasant (in flight)	5¾	85-100	175-200	1940-1971
862	Fan-Tail Pigeon	—	100-200	225-400	1940-1950
***902	Mallard	10	45-55	90-110	1940-1969
919/1	Duck	3¾	15-20	30-40	1941-1969
919/2	Duck	2⅝	10-15	20-30	1941-1969
919/3	Duck	2	5-10	10-25	1941-1969
925	Two American Blue Jays	4¾	50-60	100-120	1941-1965
926	Two Baltimore Orioles	4⅞	50-60	100-120	1941- 1965
927	Cockatoo Cardinal	6	45-50	90-100	1941-1959
928	Tanager (Western)	6	45-50	90-100	1941-1959
929	Chickadee (Chestnut backed)	5¾	45-50	90-100	1941- 1968
930	Parakeet	6	45-50	90-100	1941- 1973
980	Robin — 1st	3	10-15	20-30	1942-1973
*980	Robin — 2nd	3	9.99	RRP	1973-C
991	Chaffinch — 1st	2¾	10-15	20-30	1943-1973
*991	Chaffinch — 2nd	2¾	9.99	RRP	1973-C
992	Blue Tit — 1st	2½	10-15	20-30	1943-1973
*992	Blue Tit — 2nd	2½	9.95	RRP	1973-C
993	Wren — 1st	2¼	10-15	20-35	1943 -1973
*993	Wren — 2nd	2¼	9.95	RRP	1973-C
994	Sheldrake in flight (Taking off)	6	95-110	200-225	1943-1965
995	Sheldrake in flight (Landing)	6½	95-110	200-225	1943-1965

1015	Two Penguins (courting)	5½	70-85	140-175	1945-1966
*1018	Bald Eagle	7¼	45-50	80-100	1945-1994
1022	Two Turtle Doves	7½	125-150	250-300	1945-1969
1041	Grey Wagtail — 1st	2½	10-15	20-30	1945-1973
*1041	Grey Wagtail — 2nd	2½	9.95	RRP	1973-C
1042	Bullfinch — 1st	2½	10-15	20-30	1945-1973
*1042	Bullfinch — 2nd	2½	9.95	RRP	1973-C
*1046	Barn Owl	7¾	29·95	RRP	1946-C
1052	Barnacle Goose	6½	250-300	525-650	1946-1967
1159	Kookaburra	5¾	55-65	110-140	1949-1976
1178	Gouldian Finch (wings out)	4	55-65	110-130	1949-1959
1179	Gouldian Finch (wings in)	4	55-65	110-130	1949-1959
1180	Cockatoo (Turquoise/Pink and Pink/Grey)	8½	75-85	150-180	1949-1975
1212	Three Ducks pin tray	2¾	10-15	20-30	1951-1970
1216	Budgerigar (Blue, Green or Yellow)	7	60-70	130-140	1951-1975
1217	Budgerigar	7	60-70	130-140	1951-1970
*1218	Green Woodpecker	9	75-90	150-200	1951-1989
1219	Jay	6	125-150	250-300	1951-1970
1225	Pheasant	7¾	55-65	110-130	1951-1977
1226	Pheasant	6	55-65	110-130	1951-1977
*1383	Pigeon (blue or red)	5½	40-50	85-110	1955-1989
1413	Dove (CM series)	9	125-150	250-300	1956-1965
1415	Small Bird (CM series)	5¾	100-125	200-250	1956-1965
1416	Cock (CM series)	5	100-125	200-250	1956-1965
1420	Owl (CM series)	4¾	125-150	250-350	1956-1965
1462	Owl (CM series)	8¼	150-175	300-375	1956-1965
1467	Cock (CM series)	11¾	150-200	300-400	1956-1965
1471	Goose (CM series)	3¼	100-125	200-250	1957-1963
1482	Peacock (CM series)	3½	75-100	160-225	1957-1965
1503	Toucan	—	90-100	00-00	1957-1958
1518/1	Mallard Duck	2¾	50-75	100-150	1962-1971
1518/2	Mallard Duck	2½	50-75	100-150	1962-1971
1518/3	Mallard Duck	1⅞	50-75	100-150	1958-1971
1518/4	Mallard Duck	1⅝	50-75	100-150	1958-1971
1519/1	Mandarin Duck	1⅞	50-75	100-150	1958-1971
1519/2	Mandarin Duck	1⅝	50-75	100-150	1958-1971
1519/3	Mandarin Duck	1¼	50-75	100-150	1958-1971
1520/1	Pochard Duck	1½	50-75	100-150	1958-1971
1520/2	Pochard Duck	1¼	50-75	100-150	1958-1971
1520/3	Pochard Duck	1	50-75	100-150	1958-1971
1521	King Eider Duck	1¾	50-75	100-150	1958-1971
1522	Smew Duck	1¼	50-75	100-150	1958-1971
1523	Tufted Duck	1¼	50-75	100-150	1958-1971
1524	Goldeneye Duck	1⅝	50-75	100-150	1958-1971
1525	Goosander Duck	1¼	50-75	100-150	1958-1971
1526	Widgeon Duck	1¼	50-75	100-150	1958-1971
1527	Shelduck	1¾	50-75	100-150	1958-1971
1528	Shoveller	1⅛	50-75	100-150	1958-1971
1529	Teal Duck	1	50-75	100-150	1958-1971
1614	Fantail Pigeon	5	125-150	250-300	1959-1969
1684	Swan	3	30-35	60-75	1960-1970
1685	Swan	2	30-35	60-75	1960-1970
1686	Cygnet	1	20-25	40-45	1960-1970
1687	Cygnet	1	20-25	40-45	1960-1970
1759	Pheasant (on thick base)	5	60-70	125-150	1961-1962

1774	Pheasant (on thin base)	$4\frac{3}{4}$	50-60	100-120	1961-1975
1818	Cockatoo (turquoise/pink and pink/grey)	$11\frac{1}{2}$	100-125	200-250	1962-1973
1892	Leghorn Cockerel	9	100-125	200-240	1963-1983
1899	Sussex Cockerel	7	150-200	300-400	1963-1970
1957	Turkey (white or bronze)	$7\frac{1}{4}$	250-275	500-550	1964-1969
*2026	Owl	$4\frac{5}{8}$	14.50	RRP	1965-C
2059	Gamecock	$9\frac{1}{2}$	175-200	350-400	1966-1973
*2062	Golden Eagle (wings up)	$9\frac{1}{2}$	85-100	175-200	1966-1989
2063	Grouse (pair)	$5\frac{1}{2}$	175-200	350-400	1966-1975
2064	Partridge (pair)	$5\frac{1}{2}$	200-250	400-500	1966-1975
2067	Turkey (miniature) (white or bronze)	$2\frac{3}{8}$	45-50	90-100	1966-1969
2071	Owl (contemporary)	$5\frac{1}{8}$	40-45	80-90	1966-1967
2078	Pheasants (pair)	$6\frac{3}{4}$	175-200	375-400	1966-1975
2105	Greenfinch — 1st	3	10-15	20-30	1967-1973
*2105	Greenfinch — 2nd	3	9.95	RRP	1973-C
2106	Whitethroat — 1st	$2\frac{7}{8}$	15-20	30-40	1967-1973
*2106	Whitethroat — 2nd	$2\frac{7}{8}$	11.50	RRP	1973-C
*2183	Baltimore Oriole	$3\frac{7}{8}$	65-75	130-150	1970-1973
*2184	Cedar Wax-wing	$4\frac{5}{8}$	65-75	130-150	1970-1973
*2187	American Robin	$4\frac{1}{8}$	65-75	130-150	1970-1973
*2188	Blue Jay	$4\frac{3}{8}$	65-75	130-150	1970-1973
*2189	Black Capped Chickadee	$4\frac{1}{2}$	65-75	130-150	1970-1973
*2190	Evening Crosbeak	4	65-75	130-150	1970-1973
*2191	Quail	$4\frac{7}{8}$	65-75	130-150	1970-1973
**2238	Owl ('Moda' Range)	$6\frac{3}{4}$	40-45	80-90	1968-1971
**2239	Bird ('Moda' Range)	5	40-45	80-90	1968-1971
**2240	Cock ('Moda' Range)	6	40-45	80-90	1968-1971
*2273	Goldfinch	3	11.50	RRP	1969-C
*2274	Stonechat	3	9.95	RRP	1969-C
*2305	Magpie	5	60-75	120-150	1970-1982
2307	Eagle on Rock (wings out)	$3\frac{3}{4}$	45-50	90-100	1970-1975
*2308	Song Thrush	$5\frac{3}{4}$	60-75	130-150	1970-1989
*2315	Cuckoo	5	60-75	130-150	1970-1982
*2316	Kestrel	$6\frac{3}{4}$	50-60	100-120	1970-1989
2357	Penguin	12	200-250	400-500	1971-1975
**2359	Stork	$10\frac{1}{2}$	35-40	70-80	1971-1972
*2371	Kingfisher	5	29.96	RRP	1971-C
2398	Penguin baby standing	$6\frac{7}{8}$	150-200	325-450	1972-1975
2399	Penguin chick	$6\frac{3}{4}$	150-200	325-450	1972-1973
*2413	Nuthatch	3	9.95	RRP	1972-C
*2415	Gold Crest	$2\frac{5}{8}$	9.95	RRP	1972-C
*2416	Lapwing	$5\frac{3}{8}$	60-65	120-130	1972-1982
*2417	Jay	$5\frac{1}{8}$	60-75	120-150	1972-1982
*2420	Lesser Spotted Woodpecker	$5\frac{1}{2}$	60-65	120-130	1972-1982
2434	Penguin baby sliding	8 long	150-200	350-425	1972-1975
**2760	Pheasant	$10\frac{1}{2}$	125-150	250-300	1981-1990
3272	Tawny Owl	$3\frac{1}{2}$	9.95	RRP	1991-C
3273	Barn Owl	$3\frac{1}{2}$	9.95	RRP	1991-C
3274	Great Tit	3	11.50	RRP	1991-C
3275	Kingfisher	3	9.95	RRP	1991-C

*Available in gloss or matt finish
** Matt finish only
*** makes set of five with model No. 756
C=Current

Bird Wall Plaques

(All models carry the Beswick mark)

Model No	Name of Model	Size inches	Current Value £	$	Production Period
572	Bird on Bush	7 x 4¼	75-90	150-200	1938-1954
574	Three Blue Tits	9¾ x 5	75-90	150-180	1938-1954
596/0	Mallard	11¾	30-40	50-75	1938-1971
596/1	Mallard	10	30-35	60-70	1938-1973
596/2	Mallard	8¾	25-30	45-60	1938-1973
596/3	Mallard	7	20-25	40-50	1938-1973
596/4	Mallard	5¾	15-20	30-40	1938-1971
*658/1	Seagull	14	35-40	70-80	1938-1967
*658/2	Seagull	11¾	30-35	60-75	1938-1967
*658/3	Seagull	10⅛	25-30	50-60	1938-1967
*658/4	Seagull	8	20-25	40-50	1938-1967
*661/1	Pheasant	12	35-40	75-85	1938-1971
*661/2	Pheasant	10½	30-35	60-70	1938-1971
*661/3	Pheasant	8½	25-30	50-60	1938-1971
*705	Blue Tit (facing right)	4½	30-35	60-70	1939-1967
*706	Blue Tit (facing left)	4½	30-35	60-70	1939-1967
*707	Blue Tit (wings up)	4½	30-35	60-70	1939-1967
*729/1	Kingfisher	7½	35-40	75-90	1939-1971
*729/2	Kingfisher	6	30-35	60-70	1939-1971
*729/3	Kingfisher	5	25-30	50-60	1939-1971
731	Flamingo	15 long	150-175	325-375	1939-1955
**743	Kingfisher	6	35-40	70-80	1939-1955
*757/1	Swallow	6	30-35	60-70	1939-1973
*757/2	Swallow	5	25-30	50-60	1939-1973
*757/3	Swallow	4	20-25	40-50	1939-1973
922/1	Seagull	12	35-40	70-80	1941-1971
922/2	Seagull	10½	30-35	60-70	1941-1971
922/3	Seagull	9½	25-30	50-75	1941-1971
1023/1	Humming Bird	5¾	60-75	120-150	1945-1967
1023/2	Humming Bird	5	50-60	100-120	1945-1967
1023/3	Humming Bird	4½	40-45	75-90	1945-1967
1188/1	Pink Legged Partridge	10½	60-75	120-150	1950-1967
1188/2	Pink Legged Partridge	9	50-60	100-120	1950-1967
1188/3	Pink Legged Partridge	7½	40-45	75-90	1950-1967
1344/1	Green Woodpecker	7½	60-70	120-150	1954-1967
1344/2	Green Woodpecker	6	50-60	100-120	1954-1967
1344/3	Green Woodpecker	5	40-45	80-100	1954-1967
1530/1	Teal	8¼	70-80	150-175	1958-1967
1530/2	Teal	7¼	60-70	120-140	1958-1967
1530/3	Teal	6¼	50-60	100-120	1958-1967

* Available in gloss or matt glaze
**Pairs with 729/2 but flying in opposite direction

Butterfly Plaques

(All models carry the Beswick mark)

A small number of delightful butterfly wall plaques were modelled by Albert Hallam, early in 1957. These are difficult to find, so it would seem that only a small number were produced. They are also easily damaged and therefore collectors must pay careful attention to condition.

Model No	Name of Model	Size inches	Current Value £	$	Production Period
1487	Purple Emperor (large)	7 x 3½	175-200	350-425	1957-1960
1488	Red Admiral (large)	7 x 3½	175-200	350-425	1957-1960
1489	Peacock (large)	7 x 3½	175-200	350-425	1957-1960
1490	Clouded Yellow (medium)	5¼ x 3½	150-175	300-350	1957-1960
1491	Large Tortoiseshell (medium)	5¼ x 3½	150-175	300-350	1957-1960
1492	Swallow Tail (medium)	5¼ x 3½	150-175	300-350	1957-1960
1493	Small Copper (small)	3¾ x 2¼	125-150	150-300	1957-1960
1494	Purple Hairstreak (small)	3¾ x 2¼	125-150	150-300	1957-1960
1495	Small Heath (small)	3¾ x 2¼	125-150	150-300	1957-1960

Cats

(All current cats produced since August 1989 carry a Royal Doulton backstamp)

The Beswick collection includes all types of cats from mischievous moggies to sleek pedigrees. As seven of the Beswick modellers have been commissioned to submit cat models over the years, the cat enthusiast can acquire an interesting and stylistically varied collection. A kitten wearing a bow featured in the Beswick catalogues at the turn of the century but no more cats appeared until 1945. Since then, felines have been consistently popular.

Miss Granoska's pair of Siamese kittens, for example, which was first introduced in 1953, is still being made today. Another long term favourite is the Fireside model, also a Siamese, which was introduced in 1967. Siamese and Persians tend to be the most popular of all the breeds, certainly they are the best represented at cat shows, and this is borne out by the current collection of pedigree models.

Beswick artists have also enjoyed putting cats in humorous situations curled up on a chimney pot or playing a musical instrument and these are featured in the comic animals section.

More recently they have featured on some of the catalogue specials, along with other animals.

Model No	Name of Model	Height inches	Current Value £	$	DA No	Production Period
ø1030	Cat	6¼	35-40	70-80		1945-1973
ø1031	Cat	4½	30-35	60-70		1945-1973
***1296	Siamese Kittens	2¾	9·95	RRP	122	1953-C
ø1316	Persian Kittens	3½	35-40	70-80		1953-1973
1412	Cat (CM series)	9⅝	125-150	250-300		1956-1965
1417	Kitten (CM series)	5⅝	100-125	200-250		1956-1965
1435	Cat	5¼	85-95	175-200		1956-1961
ø1436	Kitten	3¼	7·50	RRP	123	1956-C
1437	Cat — sitting (small)	—	85-95	175-190		1956-1961
1438	Cat — standing (large)	—	85-95	175-190		1956-1961
1474	Cat (CM series)	5¼	100-125	200-250		1957-1965

1541	Cat (large)	—	85-95	175-190		1958-1960
1542	Cat	—	55-65	115-140		1958-1960
1543	Cat	3	55-65	115-140		1958-1960
***1558	Siamese lying	7¼	14·95	RRP	124	1958-C
***1559	Siamese lying	7¼	14·95	RRP	125	1958-C
*1560	Cat	10¾	75-90	150-180		1958-1966
*1561	Cat	10¾	75-90	150-180		1958-1966
**1677	Cat climbing (part of set see 1678 Wild Animals)	7½	10·95	RRP		1960-C
1803	Cat singing (part of Bedtime Chorus set see Figures)	1½	45-50	90-100		1962-1971
1857	Kitten climbing	—	45-50	90-100		1963-1964
ø1867	Persian Cat sitting	8½	23-25	RRP	126	1963-C
ø1876	Persian Cat (Prone)	3½	85-95	175-190		1963-1971
ø1877	Persian Cat	6½	85-95	175-190		1963-1971
ø1880	Persian Cat	5¼	85-95	175-190		1963-1971
***1882	Siamese Cat	9½	35-40	70-80	127	1963-1994
ø1883	Persian Cat	6½	75-85	150-160		1963-1971
ø1885	Persian Kitten	4¾	65-75	130-150		1963-1972
ø1886	Persian Kitten	4	9.95	RRP	128	1963-C
***1887	Siamese Cat sitting	4⅛	9.95	RRP	129	1963-C
***1897	Siamese Cat standing	6½	19·95	RRP	130	1963-C
***1897	Cat (black)	6½	20-25	40-50	131	1987-1994
ø1898	Persian Cat standing	5	20-25	40-50	132	1963-1994
***2139	Siamese Fireside Cat (sitting)	13¾	65	RRP	83	1967-C
2301	Cat climbing (part of set see 2302 Wild Animals)	4½	30-35	60-70		1970-1971
2311	Siamese Cat	1½	45-50	90-100		1970-1971

C=Current
*Available facing left or right and decorated white (Zodiac signs) or black (plain). Also available as a lamp.
**Currently still carries a Beswick backstamp.
***Available in gloss or matt finish
ø Can be found in grey, white or ginger with gloss or matt finish.
Also in tabby 'Swiss-roll' and ginger 'Swiss roll', gloss finish only
Note: The distinctive 'Swiss roll' decoration only appears to have been available from the mid to late 1960s. It is interesting to note that for one year only, 1965, the following were available in blue: 1867/1876/1877/1880/1883/1885/1886/1898.

Connoisseur Series

(All current models carry a Royal Doulton backstamp)

The models in this series of animal and bird studies form a highly specialised branch of the potters art, with a long and distinguished tradition to follow.

The series falls into five distinct groups — Cattle, Horses, Dogs, Wildlife Animals and Birds — and most of these are available on a polished wood base with an inscribed metal plate giving a description of the model and all have a matt finish, except 2431, which is gloss only.

Each piece represents a completely natural study and captures all the grace, strength and bearing of the real animal or bird portrayed. Every muscle, feather and feature is accurate and the finished models are a tribute to the

skills and knowledge of the John Beswick Studio sculptors and artists.
The series was introduced in 1967 with a very detailed model of the racehorse 'Arkle' (2065) owned by Anne, Duchess of Westminster and trained by Mr T. Dreaper in Ireland. The horse was mounted on a hardwood base and was the forerunner of many more finely detailed models.

The success of this initial model prompted Beswick to widen the scope of the series and a number of models, already in production, were then added to the series, wood bases being used as appropriate.

Model No	Name of Model	Height inches	Current Value £	$	DA No	Production Period
***998	Elephant	10¼	150-175	300-350		1943-1975
*1265	Arab Xayal Horse	7⅛	65-70	130-150		1952-1989
*1363	Hereford Bull	5⅜	100-110	200-225		1955-1975
*1564	Racehorse	12⅛	80-100	150-200		1959-1980
***1702	Puma tawny	8½	80-100	175-200		1960-1989
*1734	Hunter dapple	12⅛	90-100	180-200		1961-1983
***1770	Indian Elephant	12	150-175	300-350		1961-1982
*1771	Arab dapple	8⅛	90-100	175-200		1961-1989
*1772	Thoroughbred Horse	8⅞	65-75	130-150		1961-1989
*1933	Beagle	5⅞	65-75	130-150		1964-1989
*2045	Basset Hound	5⅞	65-75	130-175		1965-1989
***2062	Golden Eagle	9½	85-100	175-200		1966-1989
*2065	'Arkle' racehorse	11⅞	149·00	RRP	15	1966-C
*2084	'Arkle' Pat Taaffe up	12⅝	200-250	400-450		1966-1980
*2210	Highwayman on horse	13⅞	500-600	1000-1200		1968-1975
*2269	Arab Stallion with authentic saddle	9½	300-350	600-700		1969-1973
*2275	Bedouin Arab on horse	11½	500-600	1000-1400		1969-1973
***2309	Shire Horse	10¾	50-75	100-150		1970-1982
*2340	'Cardigan Bay' racehorse	9¼	350-400	750-850		1970-1976
*2345	'Nijinsky' racehorse	11⅛	149·00	RRP	16	1970-C
*2352	'Nijinsky' — Lester Piggott up	12⅝	225-275	450-600		1971-1982
*2422	'Mill Reef' racehorse	9	80-100	160-200		1972-1989
*2431	Mountie Stallion	10	300-350	600-750		1972-1975
*2463	Charolais Bull	5⅜	100-110	220-225		1975-1979
*2466/ 2536	'Black Beauty' & foal	7¾	79.95	RRP	17	1973-C
*2510	'Red Rum' racehorse	12½	149.00	RRP	18	1974-C
*2511	'Red Rum' — Brian Fletcher up	13	225-275	450-550		1974-1983
*2535	'Psalm' Ann Moore up	12¾	200-250	450-525		1975-1982
*2540	'Psalm' racehorse	11½	175-200	350-400		1975-1982
*2541	Welsh Mountain Pony	9	175-200	350-400		1975-1989
*2542	Hereford Bull	7½	129.00	RRP	19	1975-C
2554	Lion on rock	8¼	70-80	150-175		1975-1983
*2558	'Grundy' racehorse	11¼	149·00	RRP	20	1976-C
*2562	Lifeguard on horse	14½	395·00	RRP	22	1976-C
*2574	Polled Hereford Bull	7½	129·00	RRP	21	1976-C
*2580	Friesian Bull	7⅜	129·00	RRP	23	1976-C
*2581	Collie	8¼	65-75	130-150	00-00	1976-1994
*2582	Blues and Royals (mounted)	14½	395·00	RRP	25	1987-C
*2587	Alsatian	8⅞	65-75	130-150	26	1977-1994

*2600	Charolais Bull	7½	129·00	RRP	27	1977-C
*2605	Morgan Horse	11½	129·00	RRP	28	1977-C
2607	Friesian Cow	7½	129·00	RRP	29	1977-C
*2607/						
2690	Friesian Cow & calf	7½	149·00	RRP	30	1980-C
*2608	'The Minstrel' racehorse	13½	149·00	RRP	31	1978-C
**2629	Stag	13½	159·00	RRP	32	1978-C
*2648/						
2652	Charolais Cow & calf	7¼	149·00	RRP	33	1979-C
*2667/						
2669	Hereford Cow & calf	7	149·00	RRP	34	1980-C
2671	'Moonlight' horse	11¼	125.00	RRP	35	1980-C
2671	'Sunburst' horse	11¼	125.00	RRP	36	1986-C
**2671	'Nightshade' horse	11¼	159.00	RRP	35	1986-C
*2674	'Troy' racehorse	11¾	149·00	RRP	37	1980-C
**2725	Cheetah on rock	6½	85-100	175-200	39	1981-1994
**2760	Pheasant	10½	125-150	250-300	38	1981-1994

* *Mounted on polished wooden base.*
**On wooden base from 1990*
***Available in gloss or matt*

NOTES:

2629	*Stag is now called Majestic Stag*
2671	*Nightshade is now called Champion*
2725	*Cheetah on Rock is now called The Watering Hole*
2760	*Pheasant is now called Open Ground*
	(all with re-modelled bases)

Colin Melbourne Models

Beswick were always interested in new ideas and when Mr Melbourne visited the factory, in 1955, he talked to Mr Ewart Beswick, Chairman and Managing Director, about his ideas on 'modern' ceramics.

Ewart offered him employment and this gave him the opportunity to design and model a contemporary collection.

He was given his own studio and showroom within the factory and this included a special decorating and glazing department. The collection which followed was approved by the Design Council and were known as the 'CM Series)' and intended to match the contemporary scene.

Despite being of limited commercial success, these very good sculptural forms were well produced and offered at very competitive prices.

Model No	Name of Model	Size inches	Current Value £	$	Production Period
1409	Bison (large)	10½	125-150	250-300	1956-1963
1410	Cow	7⅛	100-125	200-250	1956-1961
1411	Horse	8¾	100-125	200-250	1956-1971
1412	Cat (large)	9⅝	125-150	250-300	1956-1965
1413	Dove	9	125-150	250-300	1956-1965
1414	Bison (medium)	8¾	100-125	200-250	1956-1970
1415	Bird (small)	5¾	100-125	200-250	1956-1965
1416	Cockerel (small)	5	100-125	200-250	1956-1965
1417	Kitten	5⅝	100-125	200-250	1956-1965

1418	Fox (small)	8 long	100-125	200-250	1956-1970
1419	Lion	5¼	100-125	200-250	1956-1962
1420	Owl (small)	4¾	125-150	250-300	1956-1965
1462	Owl (large)	8¼	150-175	300-350	1956-1965
1463	Bulldog	3¾	100-125	200-250	1956-1963
1465	Zebra	6	100-125	200-250	1956-1970
1467	Cockerel (large)	11¾	150-200	300-350	1956-1965
1468	Bison (small)	—	100-125	200-250	1956-1970
1469	Dachshund	3¼	100-125	200-250	1957-1965
1470	Clown on horse (small)	5¾	125-150	250-300	1957-1963
1471	Goose	3¼	100-125	200-250	1957-1963
1472	Poodle	5¾	100-125	200-250	1957-1963
1473	Pig	2½	75-100	150-200	1957-1966
1474	Cat (small)	5¼	100-125	200-250	1957-1965
1475	Fox (large)	10 long	100-125	200-250	1957-1970
1476	Clown on horse (large)	8½	150-200	300-350	1957-1963
1481	Reindeer	5½	100-125	200-250	1957-1970
1482	Peacock	3½	75-100	150-200	1957-1965

All models should be marked '<h'. Several different styles of decoration will be found for each piece.

Dogs

(All current models carry a Beswick backstamp unless allocated a 'DA' number. These are backstamped Royal Doulton)

There is no doubt that the dog is man's best friend whether it be as a hunter, guard or, most commonly, a companion. Always ready for a game or a walk and only asking for food and a bed, he amply repays all the love and attention given to him.

As early as 1898, Beswick had introduced models of dogs as mantlepiece ornaments. These Old English Dogs are still made today and are very popular. Since 1934, over a hundred dogs have appeared in the pattern books from frisky mongrels to pedigree show dogs. According to the Kennel Club there are approximately seventy different species of dog and about two hundred varieties in all, so there is still plenty of scope for the Beswick modellers.

A problem with selecting a champion dog is that breeders have different conceptions of the true characteristics of a winner or top dog, thus it is a challenge to achieve a model which is approved by all. The very best of the championship winners are singled out to pose for Beswick, with a team of experts advising on the final product. Crufts judges, for example, assess the clay reproduction and suggest improvements until satisfied that the 'conformation' is exact. Few potteries can compete against such high standards.

Model No	Name of Model	Height inches	Current Value £	$	DA No	Production Period
171	Dog begging	4¾	40-50	80-90		1934-1954
286	Dog sitting	6	25-30	50-60		1934-1959
301	Sealyham plaque	7½	50-60	100-120		1935-1940
302	Sealyham	5¾	30-35	60-70		1935-1959

307	Dog plaque	—	50-60	100-125			1935-1940
†††308	Dog sitting	6	25-30	50-60			1935-1959
361	Dachshund (pointed ears)	5½	25-30	50-60			1936-1956
øø361	Dachshund (rounded ears)	5½	25-30	50-60			1956-1982
373	Dog plaque	7	50-60	100-125			1936-1940
453	Old English Sheep Dog sitting	8½	75-85	150-175			1936-1973
ø454	Dog sitting (lollopy)	4¼	25-30	50-60			1936-1969
668	Dog plaque	10 x 11	100-120	200-250			1938-1962
752	Scottie (as model 87)	—	25-30	50-60			1939-1954
753	Sealyham	—	25-30	50-60			1939-1954
810	Bulldog ash tray (sailors hat)	4	50-60	100-120			1940-1954
869	Five dogs ash tray	2	15-20	30-40			1940-1968
916	Three dogs ash tray	2	10-15	20-30			1941-1968
917	Three dogs (as 916 ash tray)	2	10-15	20-30			1941-1965
**941	Foxhound (see 2263)	2⅞	10-15	20-30			1941-1969
**942	Foxhound (see 2265)	2¾	10-15	20-30			1941-1969
**943	Foxhound (see 2264)	2⅞	10-15	20-30			1941-1969
**944	Foxhound (see 2262)	2½	10-15	20-30			1941-1969
***961	Dalmation 'Arnoldene'	5¾	25-30	50-60			1941-1993
962	Airedale 'Cast Iron Monarch'	5½	25-30	50-60			1941-1989
963	Wire-haired Fox Terrier 'Talavera Romulus'	5¾	25-30	50-60			1941-1983
964	Smooth Fox Terrier 'Endon Black Rod'	5½	75-85	150-175			1941-1968
965	Bulldog 'Basford British Mascot'	5½	35-40	70-80			1941-1989
966	Irish Setter 'Sugar of Wendover'	5¾	25-30	50-60			1941-1989
††967	Cocker Spaniel 'Horseshoe Primular'	5¾	25-30	50-60			1941-1993
968	Great Dane 'Ruler of Oubourgh'	7	30-35	60-70			1941-1993
***969	Alsatian — 'Ulrica of Brittas'	5¾	30-35	60-70			1942-1993
970	Bull Terrier (Brindle or white)	5⅝	30-35	60-70			1942-1993
971	Sealyham 'Forestedge Foxglove'	4	75-85	150-175			1942-1967
***972	Greyhound 'Jovial Rodger'	6	30-35	60-70			1942-1989
973	English Setter 'Bayledone Baronet'	5½	25-30	50-60			1942-1989
1055	Cairn Terrier with ball	4	30-35	60-70			1946-1969
1057	Spaniel running	3¾	35-40	70-80			1946-1967
1059	Pekinese begging	4¼	30-35	60-70			1946-1967
1060	Red Setter lying down	3	35-40	70-80			1946-1962
1061	Sealyham lying down	2	30-35	60-70			1946-1962
1062	Wire haired terrier walking	4	30-35	60-70			1946-1962
1202	Boxer (Brindle or brown)	5½	30-35	60-70			1950-1988
1220	English Setter (large)	8	60-65	120-140			1951-1967
1239	Dog begging (from model 1086)	2½	40-45	80-90			1952-1967
1240	Dog sitting (from model 1096)	2⅛	40-45	80-90			1952-1967
1241	Dog howling (from model 909)	1¼	35-40	70-80			1952-1967
1242	Dog barking (from model 906)	1⅛	35-40	70-80			1952-1967
1294	Poodle (black or white) 'Ebonit Av Barbette"	—	100-150	200-300			1953-1967
1299	Corgi (black & tan or fawn)	5⅝	25-30	50-60			1953-1993
†1378/1	Old English Dog	13¼	75-80	150-175			1955-1976
†1378/2	Old English Dog	11½	65-70	130-140			1955-1972
†1378/3	Old English Dog	10	69.95	RRP	89/90		1955-C
†1378/4	Old English Dog	9	35.00	RRP	91/92		1955-C
†1378/5	Old English Dog	7½	26.00	RRP	93/94		1955-C

†1378/6	Old English Dog	5½	19.95	RRP	95/96	1955-C
†1378/7	Old English Dog	3½	12.50	RRP	97/98	1955-C
****1386	Poodle (black, white, brown or honey)	3½	15-20	30-40		1955-1989
****1460	Dachshund sitting (black & tan or tan)	2¾	9.95	RRP		1956-C
1461	Dachshund begging (black & tan or tan)	4	15-20	30-40		1957-1980
1463	Bulldog (CM series)	3¾	100-125	200-250		1956-1963
1469	Dachshund (CM series)	3¼	100-125	200-250		1957-1965
1472	Poodle (CM series)	5¾	100-125	200-250		1957-1963
***1548	Labrador (black or golden)	5½	25-30	50-60		1958-1993
****1731	Bulldog 'Bosun'	2½	11.50	RRP		1960-C
****1736	Corgi	2¾	9.95	RRP		1961-C
1753	Bull Terrier	3½	65-70	130-150		1961-1971
****1754	Cocker Spaniel (liver & white or black & white)	3	11.50	RRP		1961-C
1762	Alsatian	3¼	20-25	40-50		1961-1970
****1763	Dalmatian	3½	11.50	RRP		1961-C
1786/1	Whippet (tail curved down between legs)	4½	40-45	80-90		1961-1983
1786/2	Whippet — (tail attached to back leg)	4½	30-35	60-70		1983-1989
***1791	Collie 'Lochinvar of Ladypark'	5¾	25-30	50-60		1961-1993
1792	Sheep Dog	5½	25-30	50-60		1961-1993
1814	Collie	3¼	25-30	50-60		1962-1975
1824	Small dog singing (part of Bedtime Chorus Set — see Figures)	1⅜	45-50	90-100		1962-1971
1852	Boxer	3	30-35	60-70		1962-1975
****1854	Sheep Dog	3	11.50	RRP		1962-C
1855	Retriever	3¼	25-30	50-60		1962-1975
1871	Dubonnet Poodle	4⅛	60-80	130-175		1963-1967
1872	Dubonnet Bulldog	3¾	60-80	130-175		1963-1967
1932/ 1460	Dachshund on ash tray	5	25-30	50-60		1962-1969
1933	Beagle	5	25-30	50-60		1964-1989
****1939	Beagle	3	11.50	RRP		1964-C
1944	Yorkshire Terrier	3½	35-40	70-80		1964-1975
****1956	Labrador (Golden or Black)	3¼	9.95	RRP		1964-C
1982	Staffordshire Bull Terrier 'Bandits Brintiga'	4¾	100-150	200-300		1964-1969
***1997	Pug 'Cutmil Cupie'	4½	35-40	75-90		1965-1982
****1998	Pug	2½	20-25	40-50		1966-1989
2023	Jack Russell	5	25-30	50-60		1965-1993
2037	Scottie	4½	20-25	40-50		1965-1989
2038	West Highland Terrier	4¾	20-25	40-50		1965-1993
2045	Basset Hound	5	20-25	40-50		1965-1993
2107A	King Charles Spaniel 'Blenheim' brown/white	5¼	20-25	40-50		1967-1993
2107B	King Charles Spaniel 'Josephine of Blagreaves' Black, brown & white	5¼	20-25	40-50		1967-1993
2108	Poodle 'Ivanola Gold Digger' in black or white	5¾	100-150	250-325		1967-1971
****2109	Jack Russel Terrier	2⅝	11.50	RRP		1967-C
****2112	Cairn Terrier	2¾	9.95	RRP		1967-C
***2221	St Bernard 'Corna Garth Stroller'	5¾	30-35	60-75		1968-1988

Item	Name	Size	Price		No.	Years
2232	Old English Sheep Dog	11½	60-75	120-150	84	1968-1994
****2262	Foxhound (see 944)	2½	8.75	RRP		1969-C
****2263	Foxhound (see 941)	2⅞	8.75	RRP		1969-C
****2264	Foxhound (see 943)	2⅞	8.75	RRP		1969-C
****2265	Foxhound (see 942)	2¾	8.75	RRP		1969-C
2271	Dalmatian sitting	13¾	85.00	RRP	85	1969-C
2285	Afghan Hound 'Hajubah of Davlen'	5½	20-25	40-50		1969-1993
2286	Dachshund	10½	45-50	90-100		1969-1982
2287	Golden Retriever 'Cabus Cadet'	5¾	20-25	40-50		1969-1993
2299	Doberman Pinscher 'Annastock Lance'	5¾	25-30	50-60		1970-1993
2300	Beagle sitting	12¾	100-110	200-225		1969-1982
2314	Labrador	13½	85.00	RRP	86	1970-C
2339	Poodle (black or white)	5¾	30-35	60-70		1970-1982
2377	Yorkshire Terrier	10¼	45-50	90-100	87	1971-1994
2410	Alsatian	14	85·00	RRP	88	1972-C
****2448	Lakeland Terrier	3¼	9.95	RRP		1973-C
****2454	Chihuahua	2⅞	11.50	RRP		1973-C
2929	Collie Head (on wood mount)	5¾	20-25	40-50		1986-1988
2932	Alsatian Head (on wood mount)	5¾	20-25	40-50		1986-1988
*2946	Meal Time	3½	20-25	40-50		1987-1988
*2947	Gnawing	4¼	20-25	40-50		1987-1988
*2948	Play Time	3¾	20-25	40-50		1987-1988
*2949	Juggling	3	20-25	40-50		1987-1988
*2950	Nap Time	4½	20-25	40-50		1987-1988
*2951	Caught It	2¾	20-25	40-50		1987-1988
2979	Pointer on base (gloss)	6½	65-70	130-150		1986-1987
2980	Cocker Spaniel on base (matt only)	8¼	59·95	RRP	108	1986-C
øøø2982	Pekinese	5½	19·95	RRP	113	1986-C
øøø2984	Norfolk Terrier	4	19·95	RRP	114	1986-C
øøø2985	Poodle on cushion	5	28.95	RRP	115	1986-C
2986	English Setter on base (matt only)	8½	59·95	RRP	109	1986-C
3011	English Pointer on base (matt only)	7'³⁄₄	59·95	RRP	110	1986-C
øøø3013	Dachshund	4½	19·95	RRP	116	1986-C
øøø3055	Rottweiler	5½	27.95	RRP	99	1988-C
øøø3058	Old English Sheepdog	5½	27.95	RRP	100	1988-C
øøø3060	Staffordshire Bull Terrier	4	27.95	RRP	101	1988-C
3062	Labrador on base (matt only)	6½	49·95	RRP	111	1988-C
3066	Retriever on base (matt only)	7½	59·95	RRP	112	1988-C
øøø3070	Afghan Hound	5½	27.95	RRP	102	1988-C
øøø3073	Alsatian	5¾	27.95	RRP	103	1988-C
øøø3080	Shetland Sheepdog	5	25.00	RRP	117	1988-C
øøø3081	Boxer	5½	27.95	RRP	104	1988-C
øøø3082	Cairn Terrier	4½	19·95	RRP	118	1988-C
øøø3083	Yorkshire Terrier	5	19·95	RRP	119	1988-C
øøø3121	Doberman	5¼	27.95	RRP	105	1989-C
øøø3129	Rough Collie	5½	27.95	RRP	106	1989-C
øøø3135	Springer Spaniel	5	27.95	RRP	107	1989-C
3149	West Highland Terrier white	5	19·95	RRP	120	1989-C
3155	Cavalier King Charles Spaniel	5	35.00	RRP	121	1989-C
3258	Alsatian	3¼	11.50	RRP		1991-C
3260	Rottweiler	3¼	11.50	RRP		1991-C
3262	Yorkshire Terrier	3¼	9.95	RRP		1991-C

3270	Golden Retriever	3	9.95	RRP	1991-C
3375	Pair of Hounds	2½	11.50	RRP	1993-C
3376	Pair of Golden Retrievers	2	11.50	RRP	1993-C
3377	Cocker Spaniel	3	9.95	RRP	1993-C
3378	Alsatian	2½	9.95	RRP	1993-C
3379	Bulldog	2½	9.95	RRP	1993-C
3380	Jack Russell	2½	9.95	RRP	1993-C
3381	Retriever	2	9.95	RRP	1993-C
3382	Scottish Terrier	3	9.95	RRP	1993-C
3383	Pair of Cocker Spaniels	2	11.50	RRP	1993-C
3384	Pair of Bulldogs	2¼	9.95	RRP	1994-C
3385	Dalmatian	3	9.95	RRP	1994-C
3436	Cavalier King Charles Spaniel	2½	9.95	RRP	1994-C
3467	Pair of West Highland White Terriers	2	9.95	RRP	1994-C
3468	Pair of Old English Sheepdogs	2	10.95	RRP	1995-C
3475	Pair of Boxers	2¼	12.95	RRP	1995-C
3475	Pair of Rottweilers	2	12.95	RRP	1995-C

Note: *The 24 dogs numbered between 2979 and 3155 can be found with the Beswick mark and may command a higher price.*

*These six dogs were taken out of the Doulton Character Dog HN range (nos 1158, 1159, 2654, 1103, 1099 and 1097) and given Beswick numbers.
**Re-modelled 1969 with thinner tail and legs
***Available in matt 1970-1989
****Available in matt 1984-1989
øFound in at least 6 different colourways
øøAvailable in tan or black & tan
øøøAvailable in matt until 1989
†Available in left and right hand versions
††Available in golden, black, liver & white or black & white
†††Also available as a money box

Farm Animals

(All current farm animals carry the Beswick backstamp)

In order to maintain their reputation for realistic images of animals, authentic in every detail, Beswick designers have literally been 'down on the farm' for inspiration. Modellers have spent days in the field getting to know the subjects of their study in order to produce an accurate model which is a faithful representation of a champion breed. Many of the models actually carry the name of the award winning animal which inspired the artists. This is particularly true of the cattle and pigs which were modelled by Arthur Gredington. Introduced from 1952 onwards these are still very popular today, particularly among farming communities.

In recent years the champion breeds have been modelled by Graham Tongue and he recalls that the Charolais Bull which posed for his Connoisseur model in 1973 was the largest he had ever seen.

The recent pedigree bulls contrast dramatically with Beswick's first farm animal: a delightful lamb in playful mood modelled by Miss Greaves (323). This light-hearted approach can also be traced throughout the history of

Beswick animals and was revived in the Farmyard Humour collection which included a snoozing piglet on the back of the mother pig (2746) and a modern version of the traditional Staffordshire cow-creamer, Daisy the Cow (2792) both now withdrawn. These can be found in the 'Comical Animals and Birds' section.

In 1992, Beswick Collectors Circle members were able to purchase a 'red' and white Friesian bull, cow and a lying calf (2690 of the Connoisseur set) in a very limited edition of just 130 sets. These were finished in gloss and are now much sought after. It is possible that a few matt pieces were also done at the same time.

Model No	Name of Model	Size inches	Current Value £	$	Production Period
323	Lamb on base	—	75-85	150-175	1934-1954
369	Donkey on base	8	75-85	150-175	1936-1954
398	Goat	4½	30-35	60-70	1936-1954
832	Pig	3¾	25-30	50-60	1940-1971
833	Piglet	1¾	15-20	30-40	1940-1971
834	Piglet	1½	15-20	30-40	1940-1971
854	Hereford Calf	4¾	50-55	100-120	1940-1961
897	Donkey Foal (deferred see 950)	5¾	50-60	100-120	1941 only
899	Cow (deferred see 948)	5	75-85	150-175	1941 only
*901	Hereford Calf	4	35-40	70-80	1941-1967
935	Sheep	3½	20-25	40-50	1941-1971
936	Lamb	3¼	15-20	30-60	1941-1971
937	Lamb	2	10-15	20-30	1941-1971
938	Lamb	2	10-15	20-30	1941-1971
948	Hereford Cow	5	125-150	275-325	1944-1957
949	Hereford Bull	5¾	100-125	225-275	1944-1957
950	Donkey Foal	5¾	50-60	100-120	1944-1957
1035	Goat	5½	75-85	150-175	1945-1970
1036	Kid	2½	35-40	70-80	1945-1970
1248	Guernsey Cow (Horns separate)	4¼	75-95	150-200	1952-1975
**1248	Guernsey Cow (Horns moulded)	4¼	50-60	100-120	1975-1990
***1249	Jersey Calf	2¾	12·95	RRP	1954-C
***1249	Friesian Calf	2¾	12·95	RRP	1954-C
***1249	Ayrshire Calf	2 ¾	15-20	30-40	1954-1990
***1249	Guernsey Calf	2¾	15-20	30-40	1952-1990
1249	Hereford Calf	2¾	25-30	50-60	1992-1993
**1345	Jersey Cow —'Newton Tinkle'	4¼	27.95	RRP	1954-C
**1350	Ayrshire Cow 'Ickham Bessie'	5	50-60	100-120	1954-1990
**1360	Hereford Cow	4¼	27.95	RRP	1954-C
**1362	Friesian Cow ' Claybury Leegwater'	4½	27.95	RRP	1954-C
**1362	Friesian Cow (red)	4½	100-125	200-250	1992 only
**1363	Hereford Bull	4½	27.95	RRP	1955-C
øø1364	Donkey	4½	14.95	RRP	1955-C
1406	Dairy Shorthorn Calf	3	75-100	150-200	1957-1973
1406	Hereford Calf	3	40-50	80-100	1956-1975
1406	Aberdeen Angus Calf	3	45-55	90-125	1958-1975
1410	Cow (CM series)	7⅛	100-125	225-275	1956-1961
**1422	Jersey Bull 'Dunsley Coy Boy'	4½	27.95	RRP	1956-C
**1439	Friesian Bull 'Coddington Hilt Bar'	4¾	33.00	RRP	1956-C
**1439	Friesian Bull (red)	4¾	100-125	200-250	1992 only

**1451	Guernsey Bull				
	'Sabrina's Sir Richmond 14th'	4¾	50-60	100-125	1956-1990
øø1452	White Sow 'Champion				
	Wallqueen 40th'	2¾	14·95	RRP	1956-C
øø1453	White Boar 'Wall				
	Champion Boy 53rd'	2¾	14·95	RRP	1956-C
**1454	Ayrshire Bull 'Whitehill Mandate'	5¼	50-60	100-125	1956-1990
1473	Pig (CM series)	2½	75-100	175-225	1957-1966
1504	Dairy Shorthorn Bull				
	'Gwersylt Lord Oxford 74th'	5	225-275	475-575	1957-1973
1510	Dairy Shorthorn Cow				
	'Eaton Wild Eyes 91st'	4¾	225-275	475-575	1957-1973
1511	Sow 'Merrywood Silver				
	Wings 56th' Saddleback	2¾	125-150	250-300	1957-1969
1512	Boar 'Far Acre Viscount				
	3rd' Saddleback	2¾	125-150	250-300	1957-1969
ø**1562	Aberdeen Angus Bull	4½	50-60	100-125	1958-1990
ø**1563	Aberdeen Angus Cow	4¼	50-60	100-125	1959-1990
**1740	Highland Cow	5½	50-60	100-125	1961-1990
1746	Galloway Bull 'Silver Dunn'	4½	500-600	1000-1200	1961-1968
1746	Galloway Bull — belted	4½	650-750	1300-1500	1963-1968
1746	Galloway Bull (black)	4½	500-600	1000-1250	1961-1968
øø1765	Black Faced Sheep	3¼	11.50	RRP	1961-C
***1827	Highland Calf	3	15-20	30-40	1962-1990
***1827	Hereford Calf	3	12.95	RRP	1985-C
***1827	Aberdeen Angus Calf	3	15-20	30-40	1985-1990
***1827	Charolais Calf	3	12·95	RRP	1985-C
øø1828	Black Faced Lamb	2⅜	6·95	RRP	1962-C
1917	Merino Ram	4½	250-300	550-625	1963-1966
**2008	Highland Bull	5	50-60	110-130	1965-1990
øø2110	Donkey Foal	4⅜	11·50	RRP	1967-C
øø2267	Donkey	5½	16.50	RRP	1969-C
**2463	Charolais Bull (small)	5	33.00	RRP	1975-C
**2549	Polled Hereford Bull	5	55.00	RRP	1975-C
2690	Lying Calf	2¼	75-100	150-200	1992 only
****3071	Black Faced Ram	3½	16.50	RRP	1988-C
****3075	Charolais Cow	4⅞	27.95	RRP	1988-C

*Early versions have an open mouth
**Available in matt finish 1985-1989
***Available in matt finish 1987-1989
****Available in matt finish 1989 only
øSome are backstamped 'Aberdeen Angus Society'
øøAvailable in matt finish 1984-1989

Fish

(All models carry the Beswick mark)

The sport of many is to sit in quiet solitude on the bank of an equally quiet river and hope that one's knowledge and skill will land a good catch. Any one of the excellent range of fish portrayed by Beswick would be an appropriate addition to the angler's collection.

Fish studies would appear to have been a new departure for Beswick, although an old catalogue contains an illustration of a dolphin jug.

All the models are supported on a base, some balanced on their tail whilst others lie horizontally. Often the fins and tail are vulnerable to damage and it is therefore difficult to find perfect examples.

As with all Beswick animal studies, a team of experts visited Beswick to verify the accuracy of each fish model. Not only were they concerned to check the size and proportions of the fish, but as Colin Melbourne remembers, the number of scales were actually counted!

Model No	Name of Model	Size inches	Current Value £	$	Production Period
1032	Trout	6¼	60-70	130-150	1945-1975
1047	Angel Fish	7¼	100-110	200-225	1946-1966
1232	Oceanic Bonito	7¼	110-120	225-250	1952-1967
1233	Atlantic Salmon	6½	90-100	180-200	1952-1969
1235	Barracuda	4¾	90-100	180-200	1952-1967
1243	Marlin	5½	90-100	180-200	1952-1969
1246	Golden Trout	6	85-95	175-200	1952-1969
1266	Large Mouthed Black Bass	5	100-110	200-225	1952-1967
1390	Trout (small)	4	45-50	90-100	1955-1975
1485	Black Bass	6	110-120	225-250	1957-1967
1599	Trout ash bowl	5	75-85	150-175	1959-1970
1874	Roach	4¼	75-85	150-175	1963-1970
1875	Perch	4¼	75-85	150-175	1963-1970
2066	Salmon	8	90-100	175-200	1966-1975
2087	Trout	6	85-95	175-200	1966-1975
*2254	Fish ('Moda' range)	4⅝	50-60	100-120	1968-1970

*Matt finish

Horses, Foals and Ponies

(All current items in this section produced since August 1989, carry a Royal Doulton backstamp)

This is the subject for which Beswick is best known and it is the largest section of all with over 150 recorded models, 14 being continuously in production for over 35 years. The first horse (701), modelled by Arthur Gredington in 1939, was based on Bois Russell the winner of the 1938 Derby. It was innovatory as it introduced the concept of modelling from champions and named breeds. *The Pottery Gazette and Glass Trade Review* was quick to praise and appreciate John Beswick's new style. In April 1942 it wrote: ". . . among Beswick's wares were a host of splendidly modelled and lifelike animal subjects including some particularly fine horses and foals — both hunters and shires, this being a type of potting for which the firm has established a big reputation . . ."

Since Bois Russell, many famous racehorses have been immortalised by Beswick; Arkle, Grundy, Red Rum, Troy, Nijinski and Cardigan Bay being just some of the well known names among them. Until 1983 collectors could opt to have the horses ridden by equally famous jockeys such as Lester Pigott on Nijinski.

It has always been something of a gamble for the Beswick modellers to choose a horse which will continue to be as successful in the future as it has been in the past. The horse's owner is contacted and, once permission for the model is obtained, the modeller and design manager arrange a visit to study the animal. During the visit they meet and talk to all who are connected with the horse — the owner, the trainer and the grooms so that its personality can be fully understood. The horse is studied from all angles, particularly when it is at its most relaxed, paying particular attention to the pose, facial expressions, marks and, above all, its character. Sketches are made and photographs are taken to check that markings, colours and other details are accurate. Although all horses have a similar bone and muscle structure the expression and character of each is different and it is this which the modeller wishes to portray in clay. Back in the studio, the modeller starts working with the clay to put this into effect. The bone measurements and pose are positioned first and over this the rib cage and muscle structure are built up with sinews, veins, hair and mane following. In this way the physical appearance as well as the character and spirit of each horse is captured.

Throughout his work the sculptor has had to bear in mind the size of the finished model, the various methods of production, the type of decoration and the eventual price. The size is of particular importance since shrinkage of one twelfth occurs during firing. Consultations between the modeller and designer are frequent. The completed model is checked against the photographs and then the owner is invited to the factory to comment on its fidelity. One or two minor alterations are usually made as a result, and the finished, fully approved model then passes to the mould maker.

An early series of horses portrayed Mountain and Moorland ponies. In producing these, Beswick worked closely with R. S. Summerhays, a past President of the National Pony Society, who approved each model for accuracy of shape and colour. He also wrote an introduction with comments on each breed of pony for the accompanying sales brochure of the period.

Not all of Beswick's horses are based on named animals, but all must have the correct proportions and anatomical structure to maintain Beswick's high standards. Once these considerations are fulfilled, endless variations are possible.

Since 1981 Graham Tongue has romanticised the character of the horse in the 'Spirit' collection, with evocative names such as 'Spirit of Fire', 'Spirit of Freedom' and 'Spirit of Earth', the latter portraying a massive working horse. Clydesdales, Shires and Percherons have all featured in the collection over the years, some complete with leather harness.

Originally the racehorse (1564) was also available with a detachable leather saddle. The first model to actually include a rider was the Huntsman (868), which is now withdrawn. Since then a Cowboy, an Indian, a Bedouin Arab, a Canadian Mountie, a Lifeguard and a Guardsman have all appeared on horseback. The Guardsman was modelled at Kensington Barracks and it took over two hours to model the details of his uniform alone. Equally faithful in every detail are the portraits of Her Majesty, Queen Elizabeth II on Imperial, and his Royal Highness, the Duke of Edinburgh on Alamein.

To mark the Beswick Centenary in 1994, it was decided to model 'Cancara', the black horse, a Trakehner stallion. Available with a Beswick backstamp during 1994 only, it will, thereafter, carry a Royal Doulton backstamp.

With such a variety of colours used for decorating horses over the years, it is impossible here, to give all the relevant information which is needed. I suggest that you obtain a copy of Marilyn Sweets book *A Guide to Horses, Ponies & Foals* where you will find all the detail required. In the following lists, the current value given is for the 'basic' brown horse and makes no allowance for special colours. Any colour, other than brown, will command a higher price.

A model, well worth mentioning here, is 'Kruger' a Welsh Mountain Pony, the last working pit pony at the Chatterley Whitfield mine when he retired in 1931. In 1987, following the mines earlier closure, a mining museum was set up on the site and it was suggested that a model of him should be made and presented to Princess Anne, when she opened the museum on 13th October, 1987. A total of 4 were cast, one to the Princess, one to the mining museum, one to the Beswick museum and the fourth was auctioned for charity.

Financial difficulties forced closure of the mining museum in 1994 and the model was offered at auction. The price realised was nearly £2600/$5000 and this Beswick model is therefore the most valuable ever. The model was based upon Beswick Connoisseur No 2541, a Welsh Mountain Pony, and Graham Tongue, chief designer of the John Beswick Studio of Royal Doulton, recalls that he only had about two weeks in which to prepare a new model. The other interesting thing is that this is the first piece since 1934 not to be allocated a shape number.

Horses

Model No	Name of Model	Size inches	Current Value £	$	DA Number	Production Period
**701	'Bois Russell' Derby Winner 1938	8	25.00	RRP	42	1939-C
701	Up to 10 discontinued colours		30-160	60-325		
855	Horse	6	25.00	RRP	44	1940-C
855	Up to 7 discontinued colours		20-100	40-200		
**976	Mare	6¾	25.00	RRP	46	1942-C
976	Up to 8 discontinued colours		25-140	50-300		
**1182	Horse	8¾	29.95	RRP	48	1950-C
1182	Up to 10 discontinued colours		30-135	60-275		
**1261	Palomino	6¾	25.00	RRP	49	1952-C
1261	Up to 10 discontinued colours		20-130	40-160		
1265	Arab Xayal	6¼	25.00	RRP	50	1952-C
1265	Up to 7 discontinued colours		20-130	40-160		
1361	Hackney Horse	7¾	50-60	100-120		1954-1982
1361	Up to 9 discontinued colours		45-180	90-360		
1373/1	Pinto Horse (tail hanging loose)	6½	65-75	130-150		1955-1982
1373/2	Pinto Horse (tail attached to leg)	6½	55-65	110-130		1982-1990
1373	Up to 5 discontinued colours		40-120	80-250		
1411	Horse (C.M. series)	8¾	100-125	200-250		1956-1971
1484	Hunter Horse (as 1501)	6¾	40-50	80-100		1957-1982
1484	Up to 7 discontinued colours		30-125	60-250		
1516	Appaloosa	5¼	150-175	300-375		1957-1966

No.	Description	Height	Price 1	Price 2	RRP No.	Years
1516	Up to 6 discontinued colours		100-225	200-450		
1549	Horse	7½	25.00	RRP	51	1958-C
1549	Up to 9 discontinued colours		20-120	40-240		
1557	'Imperial' (modified 1546)	8¼	45-60	90-125		1958-1982
1557	Up to 7 discontinued colours		25-125	50-250		
1564	Racehorse with or without saddle	11¼	80-100	175-225		1959-1980
1564	Up to 8 discontinued colours		60-250	120-500		
1734	Hunter Horse	11¼	90-100	180-200		1961-1983
1734	Up to 8 discontinued colours		55-250	110-500		
**1771	Arab Horse	7½	25.00	RRP	52	1961-C
1771	Up to 10 discontinued colours		20-200	40-400		
1772	Thoroughbred Horse	8	25.00	RRP	53	1961-C
1772	Up to 8 discontinued colours		20-200	40-400		
1772A	Appaloosa	8	49·95	RRP	68	1961-C
1793	Welsh Cob	7½	60-70	120-150		1962-1982
1793	Up to 6 discontinued colours		30-125	60-250		
1812	Mare	5¾	25-30	50-60		1962-1990
1812	Up to 10 discontinued colours		30-100	60-200		
**1991	Mare	5½	19.95	RRP	55	1964-C
1991	Up to 9 discontinued colours		20-100	40-200		
**1992	Stallion	5½	19.95	RRP	56	1964-C
1992	Up to 9 discontinued colours		20-100	40-200		
2186	Quarter Horse	8¼	60-80	120-160		1968-1982
2186	Up to 2 discontinued colours		70	150		
2282	Norwegian Fjord Horse	6¼	250-300	500-600		1969-1975
2421	The Winner Racehorse	9¾	60-80	120-175		1972-1982
2421	Up to 2 discontinued colours		60-80	120-175		
2459	Mare lying	5	140-160	275-325		1973-1976
†2466	'Black Beauty' Horse	7⅛	39.95	RRP	65	1973-C
2671	'Moonlight' White Racehorse	11¼	125.00	RRP	35	1980-C
2671	'Sunburst' Palomino	11¼	125.00	RRP	36	1986-C
2671	'Nightshade' Black horse	11¼	90-100	180-200		1986-1989
2671	Up to 2 discontinued colours		100-125	200-250		
**2688	'Spirit of the Wind' with or without wood base	8	39·95	RRP	57	1980-C
2688	Up to 8 discontinued colours		40-60	80-120		
**2689	'Spirit of Freedom'	7	39·95	RRP	58	1980-C
2689	Up to 7 discontinued colours		40-60	80-120		
**2703	'Spirit of Youth' (same model as 2466)	6½	39·95	RRP	59	1981-C
		7	49·95	RRP		1981-C
2703	Up to 7 discontinued colours		40-60	80-120		
**2829	'Spirit of Fire'	8	35-50	75-125	60	1983-1994
2829	Up to 7 discontinued colours		40-60	80-120		
†2916	'Spirit of Peace' lying	5	49.95	RRP	63	1985-C
2916	Up to 7 discontinued colours		50-60	100-120		
†2935	'Spirit of Nature'	5½	49·95	RRP	73	1985-C
2935	Up to 7 discontinued colours		50-60	100-120		

Foals

No.	Description	Height	Price 1	Price 2	RRP No.	Years
728	Foal	5	20-25	40-50		1939-1971
728	Up to 7 discontinued colours		20-50	40-100		
763	Foal (re-modelled 1956)	3¼	15-20	30-40		1939-1976
763	Up to 7 discontinued colours		20-40	40-80		
**815	Foal	3¼	9.95	RRP	74	1940-C
815	Up to 8 discontinued colours		10-40	20-80		
836	Foal (re-modelled 1958)	5	20-25	40-50		1940-1982

Number	Description	Size	Price	Price	Ref	Years
836	Up to 8 discontinued colours		20-50	40-100		
**915	Foal lying	3¼	9.95	RRP	75	1941-C
915	Up to 8 discontinued colours		15-45	30-90		
**946	Foal	3¼	9.95	RRP	76	1941-C
946	Up to 8 discontinued colours		15-50	30-100		
**947	Foal	4½	12.95	RRP	77	1941-C
947	Up to 8 discontinued colours		15-50	30-100		
951	Foal (Shire)	6¼	20-25	40-50		1941-1971
951	Up to 7 discontinued colours		30-70	60-150		
996	Foal	3¼	10-15	20-30		1943-1976
996	Up to 7 discontinued colours		10-35	20-70		
**997	Foal	3¼	9.95	RRP	78	1943-C
997	Up to 8 discontinued colours		10-35	20-70		
**1034	Shetland Foal	3¾	9.95	RRP	79	1945-C
1034	Up to 2 discontinued colours		15-20	30-40		
1053	Foal (Shire)	5	20-25	40-50		1946-1982
1053	Up to 8 discontinued colours		20-60	40-80		
1084	Foal	4½	20-25	40-50		1947-1982
1084	Up to 8 discontinued colours		20-50	40-100		
1085	Foal	3½	20-25	40-50		1947-1971
1085	Up to 7 discontinued colours		20-60	40-120		
**1407	Foal	4½	9.95	RRP	80	1956-C
1407	Up to 8 discontinued colours		15-40	30-80		
**1813	Foal	4½	9.95	RRP	81	1962-C
1813	Up to 7 discontinued colours		15-40	30-80		
**1816	Foal	3⅜	9.95	RRP	82	1962-C
1816	Up to 8discontinued colours		15-40	30-80		
1817	Foal	3¼	15-20	30-40		1962-1975
1817	Up to 6 discontinued colours		20-40	40-80		
2460	Foal lying	3½	70-80	150-175		1973-1976
†2536	'Black Beauty' Foal	5⅞	18.95	RRP	66	1975-C
2536	Up to 4 discontinued colours		15-25	30-50		
†2837	'Springtime' (foal)	4	18.95	RRP	69	1983-C
		4½	23.95	RRP		1983-C
2837	Up to 3 discontinued colours		20-25	40-50		
†2839	'Young Spirit' (foal)	4	18.95	RRP	70	1983-C
		4½	23.95	RRP		1983-C
2839	Up to 3 discontinued colours		20-25	40-50		
†2875	'Sunlight' (foal)	4	18.95	RRP	71	1983-C
		4½	23.95	RRP		1985-C
2875	Up to 3 discontinued colours		20	40		
†2876	'Adventure' (foal)	4	18.95	RRP	72	1983-C
		4½	23.95	RRP		1985-C
2876	Up to 3 discontinued colours		20	40		

Horses on Bases

Number	Description	Size	Price	Price	Ref	Years
766	Foal (on or off base)	3¾	75-100	175-225		1939-1954
953	Mare & Foal	7¾	80-100	175-220		1941-1983
953	Up to 7 discontinued colours		60-225	120-450		
1014	Prancing Horse	10¼	60-70	120-150		1945-1990
1014	Up to 10 discontinued colours		75-200	150-400		
1374	Galloping Palomino	7½	125-150	250-315		1955-1975
1374	Up to 3 discontinued colours		125-200	250-400		
1811	Bay Mare & Foal	6	80-100	160-200		1962-1973
1811	Up to 1 discontinued colour		80-100	160-200		
1918	Pony ash tray (model 1643)	11 x 8	80-100	160-200		1963-1972
2065	'Arkle' Racehorse	11⅞	149·00	RRP	15	1966-C

2137	Tang Horse	8	175-200	350-400		1967-1972
2205	Tang Horse	13	275-325	550-650		1968-1972
2242	Arab Horse	8½	150-200	300-400		1968-1975
2269	Arab Stallion with saddle	9½	500-600	1000-1200		1969-1973
2340	'Cardigan Bay'Racehorse	9¼	350-400	750-825		1970-1976
2345	'Nijinsky' Racehorse	11⅛	149·00	RRP	16	1970-C
2422	'Mill Reef' Racehorse	9	80-100	160-200		1972-1989
2431	Mountie Stallion	10	300-350	625-750		1972-1975
2510	'Red Rum' Racehorse	12	149·00	RRP	18	1974-C
2540	'Psalm' Racehorse	11½	175-200	350-400		1975-1982
2541	Welsh Mountain Pony	9	175-200	350-400		1975-1989
2558	'Grundy' Racehorse	11¼	149·00	RRP	20	1976-C
2605	Morgan Horse	11½	229·00	RRP	28	1977-C
2608	'The Minstrel' Racehorse	13¼	149·00	RRP	31	1978-C
2674	'Troy' Racehorse	11¾	149·00	RRP	37	1980-C
**2688	'Spirit of the Wind'	8	39.95	RRP	57	1980-C
**2689	'Spirit of Freedom'	7	39.95	RRP	58	1980-C
†2689	'Spirit of Affection' – Black					
&2536	Beauty Foal & Spirit of Freedom together	7	65·00	RRP	64	1980-C
2689&2536	Up to 3 discontinued colours		75-95	150-200		
**2703	'Spirit of Youth' (same model as 2466)	6½	39.95	RRP	59	1981-C
		7	49.95	RRP		1981-C
**2829	'Spirit of Fire'	8	35-50	75-125	60	1983-1994
†2837	'Springtime' (foal)	4	18.95	RRP	69	1983-C
†2839	'Young Spirit' (foal)	4	18.95	RRP	70	1983-C
†2875	'Sunlight' (foal)	4	18.95	RRP	71	1983-C
†2876	'Adventure' (foal)	4	18.95	RRP	72	1983-C
2914	'Spirit of Earth'	7¾	40-50	80-100	61	1985-1993
2914	Up to 5 discontinued colours		55-65	110-130		
†2916	'Spirit of Peace' lying	5	49.95	RRP	63	1985-C
†2935	'Spirit of Nature'	5½	49·95	RRP	73	1985-C
3021	Cream Unicorn on china base (very limited issue. Special Commission)	9¼	175-200	350-400		1987 only
3426	'Cancara'	15¼	250.00	RRP	234	1994-C

Mounted Horses

868	Huntsman on rearing horse on base (re-modelled 1952)	10	80-100	175-225		1940-1994
868	Up to 9 discontinued colours		100-300	200-600		
939	Girl on horse jumping fence on base (horse as model 982)	9¾	150-175	300-350		1941-1962
982	Side saddle lady on horse jumping fence on base. (Horse as model 939)	10	150-175	300-375		1942-1967
1037	Horse & Jockey	8½	175-200	375-400		1945-1976
1145	15th Century Knight in armour, mounted on horse	10¾	750-850	1500-1775		1949-1969
1375	Canadian Mountie	8¼	225-275	450-600		1955-1976
1377	Mounted Cowboy	8¾	300-350	600-725		1955-1969
1391	Mounted Indian	8½	175-200	375-425		1955-1990
1499	Girl on Pony	5½	110-130	220-275		1957-1976
1499	Up to 3 discontinued colours		120-200	240-400		
1500	Boy on Pony	5½	110-130	220-275		1957-1976
1500	Up to 3 discontinued colours		120-200	240-400		

No.	Description	Size					Years
1501	Huntsman	$8\frac{1}{4}$	80-100	160-200			1957-1994
1501	Up to 7 discontinued colours		80-300	160-600			
1546	H.M. Queen Elizabeth II						
	on 'Imperial'	$10\frac{1}{2}$	175-225	350-450			1958-1980
1588	H.R.H. Duke of						
	Edinburgh on 'Alamein'	$10\frac{1}{2}$	175-225	350-450			1958-1980
1624	Mounted Lifeguard of the						
	Household Cavalry	$9\frac{1}{2}$	250-300	525-650			1959-1977
1730	Huntswoman	$8\frac{1}{4}$	80-100	160-200			1960-1994
1730	Up to 5 discontinued colours		80-300	160-600			
1862	Horse & Jockey	8	175-200	375-425			1963-1982
1862	Up to 1 discontinued colour		175-200	375-425			
2084	'Arkle' Racehorse on wood						
	base Pat Taaffe up	$12\frac{5}{8}$	200-250	425-525			1966-1980
2210	Highwayman on rearing horse						
	(Base set in wood stand)	$13\frac{7}{8}$	500-600	1100-1300			1968-1975
2275	Mounted Bedouin Arab						
	(Base set in wood stand)	$11\frac{1}{2}$	500-600	1000-1250			1969-1973
2352	'Nijinsky' Racehorse on wood						
	base. Lester Piggott up	$12\frac{5}{8}$	225-275	450-550			1971-1982
2467	Lippizzaner with Rider						
	on round or oval base	10	300-350	600-700			1973-1980
2505	Steeplechaser on base	$8\frac{3}{4}$	300-350	600-700			1974-1980
2511	'Red Rum' Racehorse						
	on wood base B. Fletcher Up	$12\frac{1}{4}$	225-275	450-575			1974-1983
2535	'Psalm' Racehorse						
	on wood base Anne Moore Up	$12\frac{3}{4}$	200-250	425-525			1975-1982
2562	Life-Guard on horseback						
	on wood base	$14\frac{1}{2}$	395.00	RRP	22		1976-C
2582	Blues and Royals on						
	horseback on wood base	$14\frac{1}{2}$	395.00	RRP	25		1987-C

Heavy Horses

No.	Description	Size					Years
818	Shire with or without harness	$8\frac{1}{2}$	29.95	RRP	43		1940-C
818	Up to 11 discontinued colours		35-200	70-400			
818	Shire (black)						
	(Collectors Special)	$8\frac{1}{2}$	200-250	425-525			1990 only
975	Trotting Horse (Shire)	$8\frac{3}{4}$	35.00	RRP	45		1942-C
975	Up to 8 discontinued colours		30-175	60-350			
1050	Shire Horse grazing	$5\frac{1}{2}$	50-60	100-120			1946-1971
1050	Up to 6 discontinued colours		85-200	170-400			
1359	'Hasse Dainty' Suffolk Punch	8	125-150	250-300			1954-1971
1359	Up to 1 discontinued colours		180	360			
2309	'Burnham Beauty' (Shire Horse						
	also in working harness)	$10\frac{3}{4}$	50-75	100-175			1970-1982
2309	Up to 2 discontinued colours		80-120	160-240			
2464	Percheron in show harness	$9\frac{3}{4}$	200-250	400-500			1973-1982
2465	Clydesdale in show or						
	working harness	$10\frac{3}{4}$	175-225	375-475			1973-1982
2548	Small Shire	6	250-300	500-600			1976 only
†2578	Shire Horse with or						
	without working harness	$8\frac{1}{4}$	75.00	RRP	62		1976-C
2578	Up to 3 discontinued colours		75-115	150-230			
**2914	'Spirit of Earth'	7	40-50	80-100	61		1985-1993
2914	Up to 5 discontinued colours		55-65	110-130			

Ponies

No	Name	Size				Dates
1033	Shetland Pony	5¾	19.95	RRP	47	1945-C
1033	Up to 5 discontinued colours		30-150	60-300		
1197	Pony head up	5½	30-35	60-70		1950-1972
1197	Up to 9 discontinued colours		30-150	60-300		
1480	Pony (as 1500)	4	75-95	150-200		1957-1966
1480	Up to 6 discontinued colours		50-125	100-250		
1483	Pony (as 1499)	5	75-95	150-200		1957-1966
1483	Up to 7 discontinued colours		50-125	100-250		
1641	Connemara Pony 'Terese of Leam'	7	80-100	160-200		1959-1983
1642	Dartmoor Pony 'Jentyl'	6¼	50-60	100-125		1959-1983
1643	Welsh Mountain Pony 'Coed Coch Madog'	6¼	80-100	160-200		1959-1989
1644	Highland Pony 'Mackinonneach'	7¼	60-70	120-150		1959-1989
1644	Up to 1 discontinued colours		150	300		
1645	Exmoor Pony 'Heatherman'	6½	50-60	100-125		1959-1984
1646	New Forest Pony 'Jonathan 3rd'	7	50-60	100-125		1960-1983
1647	Fell Pony 'Dene Dauntless'	6¾	50-60	100-125		1960-1982
1648	Shetland Pony 'Eschon Chan Ronay'	4¾	40-45	80-90		1960-1989
1671	Dales Pony 'Maisie'	6½	50-60	100-120		1960-1982
2468	Icelandic Pony	—	250-300	500-600		1973-1974

Wall Plaques of Horses

No	Name	Size			Dates
686	Horse's Head through a horseshoe looking left	7¼ x 6	50-60	100-125	1939-1940
687	Horse's Head through a horseshoe looking right	7¼ x 6	50-60	100-125	1939-1940
806	Horse's Head Plaque (as 686 with raised back)	7¼ x 6	50-60	100-125	1940-1967
807	Horse's Head Plaque (as 687 with raised back)	7¼ x 6	50-60	100-125	1940-1967
1382	Hunter Horse Head	4 x 4	35-40	70-80	1955-1969
1384	Palomino Horse Head	4 x 4	35-40	70-80	1955-1969
1385	Arab Horse Head	4 x 4	35-40	70-80	1955-1969
1505	Huntsman (as 868) Plaque	10	100-125	200-250	1957-1962
1513	Lady on horse 'taking off'	9 x 4¼	100-125	200-250	1957-1962
1514	Man on horse 'landing'	8¾ x 7¾	100-125	200-250	1957-1962
1515	Lady on horse 'going over'	8 x 5½	100-125	200-250	1957-1962
2699	'Troy' (head only) on wood	6	20-25	40-50	1980-1989
2700	'Arkle' (head only) on wood	6	20-25	40-50	1980-1989
2701	'The Minstrel' (head only) on wood	6	20-25	40-50	1981-1989
2702	'Red Rum' (head only) on wood	6	20-25	40-50	1981-1989

Carries a Beswick backstamp for 1994 only, thereafter the Royal Doulton mark will be used.
**Higher price for matt finish*
† Current models matt only

Wild Animals

(All current Wild Animals carry a Beswick backstamp)

A trip to the zoo is an exciting day out for all the family and it would appear that the Beswick modellers have also been frequent visitors. The Lion and the Cheetah in the Connoisseur series were both modelled from animals at Dudley Zoo and the Panda (2613) was based on Chi-Chi at London Zoo.

There are over one hundred and thirty different models of which the largest and most spectacular must surely be the Indian Elephant with a tiger clawing its back and the smallest, the Mouse (1678). In between these there is a veritable Noah's Ark of very good quality, finely detailed animals. British wildlife and exotic species have co-existed in the collection over the years, giving animal lovers opportunities to specialise in either field. The Beswick modellers' interpretations have ranged from the cuddly Panda (1815) to realistic and superbly detailed Connoisseur models. Various different finishes have been offered in the Wild Animal collection, matt or glossy or, as in some of the earliest models, an all over blue glaze. Although these may lack the naturalism of later wild animals, they are still very appealing to collectors.

Model No	Name of Model	Size inches	Current Value £	$	DA No	Production Period
315	Squirrel on base	8¾	85-110	175-225		1935-1954
316	Rabbit on base	6¾	85-110	175-225		1935-1954
368	Frog on base	6	85-110	175-225		1936-1954
383	Seal on base	10	85-110	175-225		1936-1954
397	Monkey on base	7	85-110	175-225		1936-1954
417	Polar Bear on base	6¼	75-100	150-200		1936-1954
568	Elephant	9	75-100	150-200		1938-1954
569	Elephant	4¾	50-75	100-150		1938-1954
692	Elephant	4¼	50-75	100-150		1939-1954
696	Fawn standing on base Also in Flambé	7½	50-75	100-150		1939-1954
709	Beaver	—	50-75	100-150		1939-1954
711	Panda	4½	35-45	75-95		1939-1940
720	Panda Baby	3¾	30-40	60-80		1939-1954
721	Fawn lying on base	4½	50-75	100-150		1939-1954
738	Panda Mother	4½	35-45	70-80		1939-1954
823	Rabbit	3	10-15	20-30		1940-1971
824	Rabbit	2¼	10-15	20-30		1940-1971
825	Rabbit	1⅜	5-10	10-20		1940-1971
826	Rabbit	2	5-10	10-20		1940-1971
828/1	Elephant	6	50-60	100-125		1940-1960
828/2	Elephant	4½	45-55	90-120		1940-1960
828/3	Elephant	3	40-50	80-100		1940-1960
830	Lizard	7	50-75	100-150		1940-1954
841	Leopard sitting	6½	75-100	150-200		1940-1954
845	Zebra (black stripes on white body)	7¼	75-100	120-200		1940-1969
845	Zebra (black stripes on orange body)	7¼	100-150	200-300		1940-1958
853	Giraffe	7¼	60-80	120-175		1940-1975
954	Stag lying	5½	40-50	75-100		1941-1975

***974	Elephant	4¾	19·95	RRP	1942-C
***981	Stag	8	23.00	RRP	1942-C
ø998	Elephant	10¼	125-150	250-300	1943-1975
***999	Doe	6	19·95	RRP	1943-C
1000/1	Fawn	3¼	20-25	40-50	1943-1955
***1000/2	Fawn	3½	10·95	RRP	1955-C
1007	Squirrel standing	2¼	30-35	60-70	1944-1965
1008	Squirrel lying	1¾	20-25	40-50	1944-1965
1009	Squirrel cracking nut	4½	20-25	40-50	1944-1965
***1016	Fox standing	5½	19·95	RRP	1945-C
***1017	Fox lying	1¾	12·95	RRP	1945-C
1019	Bison	5¾	75-85	150-175	1945-1973
1021	Stoat in winter or summer coat	5½	200-250	400-500	1945-1973
1024	Hare running on base	5¼	200-250	400-500	1945-1962
1025	Hare sitting	7	200-250	400-500	1945-1962
1038	Koala Bear	3½	20-25	40-50	1945-1971
1039	Koala Bear	2¼	15-20	30-40	1945-1972
1040	Koala Bear	2¼	15-20	30-40	1945-1972
1043	Camel Foal	5	50-60	100-125	1946-1971
1044	Camel	7	75-100	150-200	1946-1972
1048	Springbok	7¼	200-250	425-525	1946-1962
1082	Leopard	4¾	50-60	100-125	1946-1975
1089	Koala Bear	3½	20-25	40-50	1947-1971
1160	Kangaroo	5¾	75-100	150-200	1949-1965
1308	Skunk	2¾	60-80	125-175	1953-1962
1309	Skunk	1½	40-50	75-100	1953-1962
1310	Skunk	2	40-50	75-100	1953-1962
1313	Bear (on all fours)	2½	45-50	90-100	1953-1973
1314	Bear standing	4½	45-50	90-100	1953-1973
1315	Baby Bear sitting	2¼	45-50	90-100	1953-1973
1409	Bison (CM series)	10½	125-150	250-300	1956-1963
1414	Bison small (CM series)	8¾	100-125	200-250	1956-1970
1418	Fox (CM series)	8 long	100-125	200-250	1956-1970
1419	Lion (CM series)	5¼	100-125	200-250	1956-1962
***1440	Fox (small)	2½	9.95	RRP	1956-C
1465	Zebra (CM series)	6	100-125	200-250	1956-1970
1468	Bison (CM series)	—	100-125	200-250	1956-1970
1475	Fox (CM series)	10 long	100-125	200-250	1957-1970
1481	Reindeer (CM series)	5½	100-125	200-250	1957-1970
1486	Tigress	4¼	50-60	100-125	1957-1975
1506	Lion (face to front)	5¼	40-50	80-100	1957-1967
1507	Lioness	4¾	40-50	80-100	1957-1967
1508	Lion Cub	3¾	30-35	60-75	1957-1967
1532	Hippopotamus	3½	75-100	150-200	1958-1966
1533	Polar Bear	4¾	75-100	150-200	1958-1966
1534	Seal	3	65-75	130-150	1958-1966
1551	Chamois	4	25-30	50-60	1958-1971
1597	Baby Giraffe	4¼	30-35	60-70	1959-1971
1631	Giraffe (large)	12	125-150	250-300	1959-1975
1678	Mouse (see 1677 Cats)	2½	5·95	RRP	1960-C
1688	Reindeer	3¾	30-35	60-70	1960-1971
ø1702	Puma, tawny, on rock	8½	80-100	165-225	1960-1989
	also in black	8½	100-120	200-250	1960-1975
1720	Indian Elephant & Tiger	12	250-300	500-600	1960-1975
***1748	Fox sitting	3	9·95	RRP	1961-C
ø1770	Indian Elephant (as model 1720)	12	150-175	300-375	1961-1982
***1815	Panda	2¼	7·95	RRP	1962-C

1823	Puma, tawny, on rock (small)	6	60-80	120-175		1962-1975
	also in black	6	80-100	160-200		1962-1975
1943	Beaver	2½	100-125	200-250		1964-1967
2089	Lion (face to side)	5½	40-45	80-90		1967-1983
ø2090	Moose	6¼	200-250	250-500		1968-1973
2093	Old Staffordshire Lion	5¾	150-175	300-350		1967-1969
2094	Old Staffordshire Unicorn	6	150-175	300-350		1967-1969
***2096	Tiger	7½	40-45	80-90		1967-1989
2097	Lioness	5¾	40-45	80-90		1967-1983
2098	Lion Cub	4	20-25	40-50		1967-1982
2182	Heraldic Unicorn on base	8½	150-175	300-350		1968-1969
2194	Racoon	4¼	150-175	300-375		1968-1973
2195	Beaver	4⅜	150-175	300-375		1968-1973
2222	Lion with crown	5¼	150-175	300-350		1968-1969
2223	Unicorn	5¼	150-175	300-350		1968-1969
øø2253	Hedgehog ('Moda' range)	3½	40-45	80-90		1969-1971
2302	Mouse (see 2301 Cats)	1¾	20-25	40-50		1969-1971
2312	Kangaroo (small)	4⅞	100-125	200-250		1970-1971
2348	Fox	12¼	100-125	200-250		1970-1983
2554	Lion	6½	40-45	80-90		1983-1994
*2613	Panda 'Chi-Chi' sitting					
	with bamboo shoot	3¾	50-55	100-125		1978-1980
øø2629	Stag	13½	159·00	RRP	32	1978-C
øø2725	Cheetah on Rock	6½	85-100	160-200	39	1981-1994
øø2933	Lion Head	6	20-25	40-50		1985-1989
øø2934	Tiger Head	6	20-25	40-50		1985-1989
øø2936	Stag Head	6	20-25	40-50		1985-1989
**2944	Panda sitting without					
	bamboo shoot	3¾	10-15	20-30		1986-1987
3009	Cheetah	5	40-45	80-90		1986-1994
3392	Badger (cub)	2	8.95	RRP		1994-C
3393	Badger (male)	2¼	12.95	RRP		1994-C
3394	Badger (female)	2¼	12.95	RRP		1994-C
3397	Harvest Mouse	2½	9.95	RRP		1994-C
3399	Woodmouse	3¼	9.95	RRP		1994-C

* For London Zoo and gloss finish only
** For WWF and matt finish only
***Available in matt finish 1985-1988
øAvailable in matt finish 1970-1972
øøMatt finish only

*New models of the Badger family **3392** to **3394***

*New models of Woodmouse **3399** and Harvest Mouse **3397***

*Rising Duck (ledt) **749** and Settling Duck **750***

*L-R Racoon **2194**, Beaver **1943**, Stoat **1021** and Beaver **2195***

*L-R Saddleback Sow and Boar **1511** and **1512**, Jersey Cow **1345**, Aberdeen Angus Bull **1562** and Black-faced Sheep **1765***

One of the elusive butterflies — the Clouded Yellow **1490**

L-R: Sitting Cat **1867** in 'Swiss-roll' tabby decoration with **1296** kittens in unusual white and grey colour. The **3138** Teapot is in black and white instead of the usual white

Three kittens — **1886** — in 'Swiss-Roll' decoration

Two comical pieces. Egg cup with Cat **2810** and Pillar Box Money Box with Cat **2805**. Both hard to find

*L-R: Quite a desirable group. **1030** in blue, **1877** 'Swiss-Roll' tabby, **1031** in white, **1883** 'Swiss-Roll' tabby, **1030** in ginger, **1031** and **1883** in grey stripe and **1876** grey stripe (lying)*

*A Colin Melbourne group containing (L-R): 2 Bisons **1409/1414**, Horse **1411**, Cock **1467**, Cat **1412**, Bulldog **1463** and Dachshund **1469***

*L-R: Honey colour Poodle **1386** — a rare colour, with the elusive Dog Reading Book **831**, brown colour Poodle **1386** and lying dog **1061***

*A fine study, in gloss, of Setter **2979***

L-R: Red Setter ***1060*** *lying,* ***1762*** *Alsatian,* ***1763*** *Dalmatian,* ***2221*** *St Bernard,* ***1944*** *Yorkshire Terrier,* ***1731*** *Bulldog and* ***1461*** *Begging Dachshund*

*Colour variations on Jersey Cow **1345**, Friesian markings on a Hereford colour, matt finish **1249** and the Guernsey cow **1248** with horns attached (left) and horns separate on the right*

*The very desirable 'Beswick Circle Special' group of Red Friesians, L-R: Bull **1439**, Cow **1362** and lying calf **2690***

L-R: **1047** *Angel Fish,* **1875** *Perch,* **1874** *Roach,* **1235** *Barracuda,* **1266** *Black Bass (large mouthed),* **1246** *Golden Trout,* **2066** *Salmon*

L-R: **2131** *Rabbit yawning;* **2103** *Pigs Laughing,* **2100** *Cat and Mouse laughing,* **2102** *Dog laughing;* **2130** *Dog praying*

Small Shire **2548**

Black Beauty and foal **2466/2536** *in gloss finish*

*A 'Royal' mounted group; L-R: Duke of Edinburgh **1588**, Lifeguard Trumpeter **1624**, Canadian Mountie **1375**, Lifeguard **2562** and Knight in Armour, The Earl of Warwick, **1145***

L-R: **982** *Lady Riding Side Saddle,* **1500** *Boy on Pony,* **2467** *Lippizaner,* **1377** *Cowboy,* **1499** *Girl on Pony and* **2505** *Steeplechaser*

The very rare Mountie Stallion **2431** *produced to commemorate the centenary of the Royal Canadian Mounted Police in 1974*

L-R: Running Hare **1024**, Fox **1016** and Sitting Hare **1025**

The very fine model of a Springbok **1048**

L-R: Camel foal **1043**, Camel **1044**, Giraffe **1631** and Baby Giraffe **853**. Both giraffes can be found with either light or dark markings

A rare Fawn **696** in Flambé and again in normal decoration

*Elephant **974** in pink and again in normal decoration, although the shade of this colour varies a great deal*

*Puma **1702** on all white base instead of mottled grey*

*Zebra **845** in two authentic colourways*

*L-R: Here we have the Skunk family **1308-1310**, two Koala Bears on a log and Penguin **450/2** in authentic and blue decoration*

*L-R: Leopard **1082**, Lion Cub **1508**, Tigress **1486** and Lioness **1507***

64

MICKEY MOUSE 1278–3⅞″

GOOFY
1281–4¼″

NANA
1301–3¼″

THUMPER
1291–3¼″

PLUTO 1280–3½″

TINKERBELL
1312–5″

WALT DISNEY FIGURES
COPYRIGHT

29

PETER PAN
1307–5″

PINOCCHIO
1282–4″

DONALD DUCK 1283–4″

SMEE
1302–4½″

MINNIE MOUSE 1289–4″

JIMINY CRICKET
1279–4″

Walt Disney Figures — Catalogue page

*Winston Churchill Character Jug **931**, complete with cover. This is sometimes missing*

*L-R: Mr Pickwick (sugar) **1118**, Henry VIII **2099**, Betsy Trotwood **2075**, Falstaff **2095**, Mr Bumble **2032**, Scrooge **372**, Little Nell's Grandfather **2031** and Mr Micawber **310***

Toby Philpot in both sizes with the Midshipman

*The Bedtime Chorus L-R: Pianist **1801**, Piano **1802**, Girl with Harp **1826**, Boy without Spectacles **1804**, Boy with Guitar **1825**, Boy with Spectacles **1805**, small cat **1803** and small dog **1824***

*A mixed group, L-R: White Mouse **1678**, Brown Mouse **1678**, Dog begging **1239**, Toby on a Barrel **1114**, Chicken sitting **2202**, Martha Gunn **1113**, Dog sitting **1240**, Dog praying **2130**, Chicken (salt) **1099** and Cat egg cup **2810***

Beatrix Potter variations L-R: Fierce Bad Rabbit (feet down) **2586/2**, *Fierce Bad Rabbit (feet up)* **2586/1**, *Mr Tod* **3091** — *quite a definite variation on the head!*

Anyone for golf? L-R: Rabbit with golf bag **665** *and Rabbit with knapsack* **624**. *Both are spillholders*

The complete set of 12 resin 'Beswick Bears', only in production for about one year

*The very desirable napkin ring **284** in two colourways*

The new 'Pig Prom' set of 6 authentic breeds carrying a Beswick Centenary badge stamp for 1994 only. Thereafter, the normal Beswick backstamp will be used

Six of the 'English Country Folk' series. L-R: The Gentleman Pig **3417**, The Hiker Badger **3421**, The Huntsman Fox **3418**, The Fisherman Otter **3419**, The Sheperd Sheepdog **3422** and The Gardener Rabbit **3420**

Two more of the 'English Country Folk' series.
*L-R: The Lady Pig **3448** and Mrs Rabbit **3447***

*Large size Jemima Puddleduck **3373** carrying a*
special Beswick Centenary backstamp for 1994 only

Some of the 'Little Loveables' grouped together. Note 'Please' on the left was a replacement for the
short-lived 'God Loves Me'

The superb 'Thunderbirds' set of six busts issued as a limited edition

*Three of the very collectable Hummel series. L-R: Shepherd Boy **914**, Farm Boy **912** and Max and Moritz **911***

A fine group of pre-war figures from the 1930s, all modelled by Miss Greaves. L-R: Girl in a Breeze **390**, *Girl with hands in muff* **391**, *Child lying* **392**, *Girl with finger in mouth* **388** *and a colour variation on Girl tasting honey* **374**

Another rare group of, this time, post-war figures, the first three by Mr Gredington and the fourth by Miss Granoska. L-R: Scotsman **1125**, *Flower Pot Man* **1123**, *Sportsman* **1096** *and Danish Girl leading pig* **1230**

74

*The very appealing 'Soldier' bookends **751***

*More figures! L-R: Lady in Ball Gown **1995**, Butcher Boy **1122**, Polish Girl with hen **1222**, Finnish Girl with duck **1247**, 'Timpsons' shoemaker **1946**, Swedish Girl with cockerel **1227** and Hiker **1094***

*Animal Kingdom. Three short-lived wall plaques, Stag, Lion and Tiger. Models **2936/2933/2934***

'Cancara' the black horse. A Beswick Centenary model with a Beswick backstamp for 1994 only

*Best of Breed. Two short-lived wall plaques, Alsatian and Collie. Models **2932** and **2929***

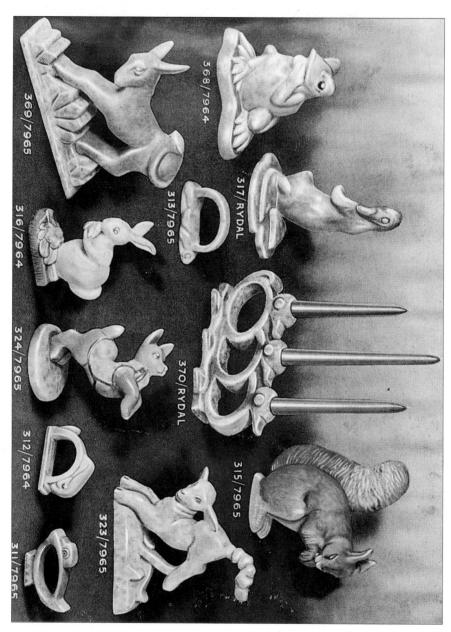

368/7964

369/7965

317/RYDAL

313/7965

316/7964

324/7965

370/RYDAL

312/7964

315/7965

323/7965

311/7965

A nice thirties group of some early decorative pieces which are very popular today

A group of the popular Beatrix Potter figures

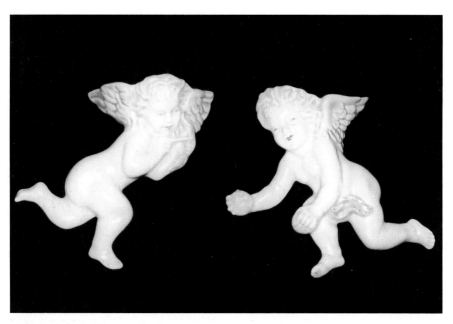

*'Cupid' wall plaques **708** and **733***

*Shakespeare plaques: As You Like It (left) **1209** and Romeo and Juliet(right) **1210***

King and Queen of Hearts from the 'Alice in Wonderland' set

L–R: **926** *Baltimore Orioles;* **929** *Chickadee;* **925** *Blue Jays*

L–R: **1226** *Pheasant;* **1022** *Doves,* **2078** *Pair of Pheasants,* **1219** *Jay,* **2063** *Pair of Grouse,* **1958** *Turkey,* **1218** *Green Woodpecker*

Part Two: Character Wares

Character and Toby Jugs, Teapots and Derivatives

(All these models carry a Beswick backstamp)

The idea of modelling a jug in the form of a human head is a very ancient one and it occurs with regularity throughout the history of ceramics. In the early 1930s there was a revival of interest in the face jug pioneered by the Royal Doulton potteries and the Beswick modellers were quick to respond to this new collecting interest. Their first character jug, **Tony Weller**, was introduced in 1935 and other Dickens personalities soon followed. During the war some patriotic character jugs were produced, promoting the endeavours of the army, navy and airforce but the Dickens theme was resumed after hostilities had ended. In 1967 two Shakespearean characters joined the throng but production was short lived.

The Beswick character jugs had all been withdrawn by 1973 but the skills of the craftsmen involved have not gone to waste. Today the Beswick studio, as part of the Royal Doulton group, is responsible for the production of all Character Jugs with a Royal Doulton backstamp.

Toby Jugs

The Toby differs from the character jug in that the whole figure is modelled into jug form not just the head and shoulders. The Toby has become a popular ornament in the drinking houses of Britain and is highly valued by many collectors. Of the six very attractive models which Beswick have produced, three are traditional types in which Toby Phillpot, a character in a popular eighteenth century drinking song, sits with a jug of ale in one hand and a tankard in the other.

The topers were soon joined by other congenial characters. **The Midshipman** playing the violin was a popular subject in the 1770s and Beswick produced a faithful version of him in 1948. The **Martha Gunn** Toby was also inspired by an eighteenth century original by Ralph Wood. She was the bathing attendant at Brighton beach who supposedly taught King George IV to swim.

Famous characters of the twentieth century have also been portrayed in Toby form and **Winston Churchill** has probably been most 'honoured' in this way. During the war Beswick introduced a very fine image of him which was only available until 1954.

All of these jugs can be classed as rare and are very hard to find today.

Derivatives

The popular Dickens personalities were not confined to character jugs. It was possible to deck out the tea table with useful Dickens wares — a **Dolly Varden** teapot with perhaps a **Pecksniff** cream jug and a **Pickwick** sugar bowl. Jam could be discreetly contained in a **Tony Weller** preserve pot and for extra spice the **Sairey Gamp** pepper pot and **Mr Micawber** salt pot could be on hand. These were all the specialities of Mr Gredington who offered alternative favourite characters.

It is doubtful whether any of these entertaining characters serve their original purpose today as they are quite popular with collectors.

Model No	Name of Model		Height inches	Current £	Value $	Production Period
281	Tony Weller (1st version)	CJ	$6\frac{3}{4}$	50-60	100-120	1935-1970
281	Tony Weller (2nd version)	CJ	7	55-65	110-120	1970-1973
310	Micawber (1st version)	CJ	$8\frac{1}{4}$	50-60	100-120	1935-1970
310	Micawber (2nd version)	CJ	$8\frac{1}{2}$	55-65	110-120	1970-1973
371	Sairey Gamp	CJ	$6\frac{1}{2}$	50-60	100-120	1936-1973
372	Scrooge	CJ	7	50-60	100-120	1936-1973
575	Laurel & Hardy cruet & base		$4\frac{1}{2}$	65-75	130-150	1938-1969
673	Tony Weller sugar		$2\frac{3}{4}$	20-25	40-50	1939-1973
674	Mr Micawber cream		$3\frac{1}{4}$	15-20	30-40	1939-1973
689	Sairey Gamp pepper		$2\frac{1}{2}$	15-20	30-40	1939-1973
690	Mr Micawber salt		$3\frac{1}{2}$	15-20	30-40	1939-1973
691	Sairey Gamp teapot		$5\frac{3}{4}$	55-65	110-130	1939-1973
735	Old Bill	CJ	5	100-150	200-300	1939-1954
736	Navy	CJ	5	100-150	200-300	1939-1954
737	Air Force	CJ	5	100-150	200-300	1939-1954
742	Panda teapot		6	75-100	150-200	1939-1954
931	Winston Churchill	TJ	7	200-225	400-475	1941-1954
1110	Toby Phillpot	TJ	8	75-85	150-175	1948-1973
1111	Toby Phillpot	TJ	$6\frac{1}{2}$	65-75	130-150	1948-1973
1112	Midshipman Toby	TJ	$5\frac{1}{4}$	125-150	250-300	1948-1973
1113	Martha Gunn holding jug	TJ	$3\frac{1}{2}$	100-125	200-250	1948-1962
1114	Toby Sitting on Barrel holding jug	TJ	$3\frac{1}{2}$	100-125	200-250	1948-1962
1116	Peggoty teapot		6	65-75	130-150	1948-1973
1117	Pecksniff cream		$3\frac{1}{2}$	15-20	30-40	1948-1973
1118	Pickwick sugar		3	15-20	30-40	1948-1967
1119	Pickwick cream		$3\frac{1}{4}$	15-20	30-40	1948-1973
1120	Captain Cuttle	CJ	$4\frac{1}{2}$	40-45	80-90	1948-1973
1121	Barnaby Rudge	CJ	$4\frac{1}{2}$	40-45	80-90	1948-1969
1129	Pecksniff sugar		$3\frac{1}{2}$	15-20	30-40	1948-1967
1203	Dolly Varden teapot		$6\frac{1}{4}$	80-100	175-225	1950-1973
1204	Mr Varden cream		$3\frac{1}{2}$	15-20	30-40	1950-1973
1205	Mrs Varden sugar		3	20-25	40-50	1950-1967
1206	Sairey Gamp preserve & lid		3	25-30	50-60	1950-1967

1207	Tony Weller preserve & lid		3	25-30	50-60	1950-1967
1369	Sam Weller teapot		6¼	100-125	200-250	1955-1973
2030	Martin Chuzzlewit	CJ	4¾	50-60	100-120	1965-1973
2031	Little Nell's Grandfather	CJ	5⅜	50-60	100-120	1965-1973
2032	Mr Bumble	CJ	4⅞	50-60	100-120	1965-1973
2075	Betsy Trotwood	CJ	5	50-60	100-120	1966-1973
2095	Falstaff	CJ	6¾	60-75	120-150	1967-1973
2099	Henry VIII	CJ	7	60-75	120-150	1967-1973
3105	Panda teapot		6	25-35	50-70	1989-1990
*3138	Cat teapot (white)		6	25-35	50-70	1989-1990
3139	Mouse teapot		7	25-35	50-70	1989-1990
3142	Squirrel teapot		7	25-35	50-70	1989-1990

CJ Character Jug   TJ Toby Jug
Small number available in black and white at a higher price

1932/1460 Dachshund ash tray

Characters from Film and Literature

(All models produced up to August 1989 carry a Beswick stamp. All current models produced since August 1989 carry a Royal Albert stamp)

Over the years, the Beswick modellers have turned the pages of many children's classics and brought a new dimension to the memorable illustrations, so that as well as enjoying the books, young readers could surround themselves with little models of their favourite characters. The timeless quality of many Victorian and Edwardian children's books makes them a fertile source of inspiration and Beswick modellers have had particular success with their interpretations of Alice in Wonderland and the tales of Beatrix Potter.

The first Beatrix Potter figure was suggested by Mrs Lucy Beswick, wife of Ewart, when she mentioned to Jim Hayward in 1947 that Jemima Puddleduck might be a good subject for a figure. When Jim Hayward took up her suggestion, copies of the Beatrix Potter tales belonging to her daughter Judith soon disappeared into the design studio. The result was so successful that a whole range of character studies from the tales of Beatrix Potter followed.

This extract from *The Publishers' Circular and Booksellers' Record* of July 1950 gives an indication of the popularity of the Beatrix Potter figures: "These little figures are creating a buying craze which is sweeping through the United States of America and Canada. This well known pottery firm first issued twelve of these charming china figures, each being about three and three quarter inches high, beautifully fashioned and coloured after the famous illustrations from Beatrix Potter's works. The colourings are full, the figures most natural and the whole present beautiful objects d'art."

Today a new figure may be suggested from the illustrations in the books — perhaps a popular character such as Peter Rabbit or Benjamin Bunny in a change of clothes or a different pose. Alternatively, the name of a character not previously illustrated such as Cottontail might suggest a study for designers in the studio. Any new ideas are discussed by the design manager and the modeller and several drawings and trial models follow. The figure must agree with the original book illustrations in every detail and so meticulous is the process that it can take six months or even longer for a model to be completed.

Following the success of the Beatrix Potter figures, Beswick started to introduce other characters from literature and film. In 1949 they introduced Zimmy the Lion, the star of **The Lion** cartoon released by the Rank Film Organisation in 1948. This character was the creation of David Hand, an ex-director at Walt Disney and such was Zimmy's success with his audience that sequel cartoons soon appeared introducing his friends Ginger Nutt, Hazel Nutt, Dinkum Platypus, Loopy Hare, Oscar Ostrich and Dusty Mole. Arthur Gredington added all these cartoon characters to the Beswick collection.

In 1952, the most famous cartoon character of all, Walt Disney's Mickey Mouse, was portrayed by Miss Granoska. Such was the popularity of Mickey and his friends that these Beswick figures are now very hard to find indeed in spite of being in production for twelve years. Also elusive are Snow White and the Seven Dwarfs which were introduced in 1954.

It was fourteen years before Beswick returned to the world of children for inspiration. Prompted by the success of Walt Disney's film version of A. A. Milne's *Winnie the Pooh*, Albert Hallam modelled a series of characters in 1968. Pooh Bear himself and Piglet must be the best known of this group along with Christopher Robin, a central character in all the books. All of these figures are now out of production and their appealing modelling makes them well worth collecting.

Another famous bear portrayed by Beswick was originally created by Mary Tourtel in 1920 but it was Alfred Bestall who popularised him in the first *Rupert Annual* published by the *Daily Express* newspaper in 1936. All of the stories and drawings in this annual were the work of Alfred Bestall who continued to write illustrated stories every year until 1973. Rupert Bear and his friends Algy Pug and Bill Badger were introduced in 1980 and have now been withdrawn.

One of the best known children's classics which has inspired the Beswick artists is *Alice's Adventures in Wonderland* by Lewis Carroll. It would seem that they referred to the original drawings by John Tenniel in the 1865 edition of this book when creating their set of eleven colourful characters. The Mad Hatter and Alice herself are particularly attractive and difficult to find.

Unlike the characters from Alice in Wonderland, Beatrix Potter and Rupert Bear, Beswick's Thelwell collection is not based on illustrations from children's stories but on a series of cartoons for *Punch* magazine. The girl and pony theme of Norman Thelwell's drawings was inspired by an incident he observed from his window. Two small podgy girls, hard hats rammed down over their ears, approached a shaggy pony well known for his uncertain temper. They calmly marched towards him, pulled his tail, cracked his nose with a crop and so made the pony their obedient servant before his astonishment had time to turn to fury. The Beswick models, first introduced in 1982 and modelled by David Lyttleton, capture the humour portrayed in Thelwell's pony cartoons.

The Beswick artists have had a long standing ability to portray character and humour and this is very much in evidence, not only in the Thelwell collection but in all their portrayals of characters from children's stories and cartoons.

Another children's classic has been interpreted by the Beswick modellers, but for various reasons the series was only available for between two and three years.

The four main characters in Kenneth Graham's story *The Wind in the Willows*, were Toad, Badger, Mole and Ratty and models of each were introduced in 1987, to be followed by Portly (Otter) and Weasel Gamekeeper in 1988. They were all withdrawn at the end of 1989.

The Royal Albert backstamp was used and each figure was allocated a model number in the Beswick pattern book. Details are given in the listings, together with the Royal Albert number.

This set came out at the same time as the decision was made, by Royal

Doulton, to change the backstamp of Beatrix Potter figures from Beswick to Royal Albert.

It is probable that this Brand name was thought to have more appeal, particularly to overseas markets.

The actual changeover date was set at 1st August, 1989, but it was obviously going to take some time for existing Beswick-marked models to clear the factory warehouse and be replaced by Royal Albert marked models.

It is believed that the highest number B.P. model to carry the Beswick mark is 3103, Tom Kitten character jug and the highest number figure to be 3094, Johnny Townmouse and Bag.

Model number 3157, Peter in the Gooseberry Net, is therefore the first B.P. model never to have carried the Beswick stamp.

In the listings, all B.P. models, from 3157 onwards, carry the Royal Albert mark and the number quoted is the Beswick pattern book model number. This number is also used in the currently published price list.

There are, however two exceptions. The large size Peter Rabbit and Jemima Puddleduck figures only carried the Beswick mark for the first year of production, thereafter changing to Royal Albert. There were also three others which due to delayed production, B.P. models 2965/66/71 were not introduced until after the backstamp changes had been made and they have therefore only carried the Royal Albert mark.

The popular Beswick gold backstamp was in use until 1970, when the brown printed transfer was substituted. It is believed that 2381 Pig Wig is the highest numbered Model to carry a gold backstamp. The gold backstamp models command a higher price.

In 1987 the three new BP character jugs models 2959/2960/3006 had a new style of backstamp where the printed word 'BESWICK' was replaced by the written words John Beswick.

In 1988 the three new BP character jugs 3088/3102/3103 and three new BP figures 3090/3091/3094 all had a different style of backstamp, where the written words John Beswick were followed by the printed words 'STUDIO OF ROYAL DOULTON, ENGLAND'.

The other three new BP figures introduced in 1988 — 2989/2996/3030 — all carried the standard printed 'BESWICK' mark. All now carry the Royal Albert stamp.

Beatrix Potter – Figures

Model No	Name of Model	Height inches	Current Value £	$	Production Period
1092/1	Jemima Puddleduck (2in short base)	4¼	35-40	70-80	1947-1988
*1092/2	Jemima Puddleduck (2¼in long base)	4¼	40-45	80-90	1988-1989
1098/1	Peter Rabbit (2in short base)	4½	35-40	70-80	1947-1988
*1098/2	Peter Rabbit (2⅜in long base)	4½	40-45	80-90	1988-1989

*1100	Tom Kitten	3½	40-45	80-90	1947-1989
*1101	Timmy Tiptoes	3¾	30-35	60-70	1947-1989
*1102	Squirrel Nutkin	3¾	30-35	60-70	1947-1989
***1103	Mrs Tittlemouse	3¾	35-40	70-80	1947-1993
1104/1	Little Pig Robinson (Blue striped smock)	4	125-140	250-275	1947-1983
*1104/2	Little Pig Robinson (Blue checked smock)	4	35-40	70-80	1983-1989
1105/1	Benjamin Bunny (left arm & slipper held away & ears protrude beyond hat)	4	150-175	300-350	1947-1979
1105/2	Benjamin Bunny (left arm & slipper flush to body & ears protrude beyond hat)	4	45-50	90-100	1979-1983
*1105/3	Benjamin Bunny (left arm & slipper flush to body & ears do not protrude)	4	35-40	70-80	1983-1989
ø1106	Samuel Whiskers	3½	40-45	80-90	1947-1989
1107/1	Mrs Tiggy Winkle (angled stripes to blouse)	3¼	65-85	130-175	1947-1975
*1107/2	Mrs Tiggy Winkle (vertical stripes to blouse)	3¼	35-40	70-80	1975-1989
*1108	Tailor of Gloucester	3¾	30-35	60-70	1948-1989
***1109	Timmy Willie	3	30-35	60-70	1948-1993

*'Mrs Tittlemouse at her doorstep' plaque **2685** and Beatrix Potter figure Diggory Diggory Delvet **2713***

Ref	Name	Size			Years
1157/1	Jeremy Fisher (spotted body)	3	65-75	130-150	1949-1979
*1157/2	Jeremy Fisher (striped body)	3	35-40	70-80	1979-1989
*1183	Lady Mouse	4	40-45	80-90	1950-1989
*1198	Hunca Munca	$2\frac{3}{4}$	35-40	70-80	1950-1989
*1199	Mrs Ribby	$3\frac{1}{2}$	35-40	70-80	1950-1989
1200/1	Mrs Rabbit (brolly sticks out)	$4\frac{1}{4}$	175-200	350-400	1950-1983
*1200/2	Mrs Rabbit (brolly flush to body)	$4\frac{1}{4}$	40-45	80-90	1983-1989
*1274	Flopsy, Mopsy & Cottontail	$2\frac{3}{4}$	35-40	70-80	1952-1989
*1275	Miss Moppet	3	40-45	80-90	1952-1989
***1276	Johnny Townmouse	$3\frac{1}{2}$	25-30	50-60	1952-1989
*1277	Foxy Whiskered Gentleman	5	50-60	100-125	1952-1989
1348/1	Tommy Brock (spade handle above hand)	$3\frac{1}{2}$	150-175	300-350	1954-1979
*1348/2	Tommy Brock (spade handle flush with hand)	$3\frac{1}{2}$	40-45	80-90	1979-1989
1355	Duchess (see also 2601)	$3\frac{3}{4}$	1500-1800	3000-4000	1954-1967
1365/1	Pigling Bland (dark mauve jacket and $1\frac{5}{8}$in dia base)	$4\frac{1}{4}$	150-175	300-350	1955-1980
*1365/2	Pigling Bland (pale violet jacket and $1\frac{7}{8}$in dia base)	$4\frac{1}{4}$	40-45	80-90	1980-1989
*1545	Old Woman Who Lived in a Shoe	$2\frac{1}{2}$	35-40	70-80	1958-1989
*1675	Goody Tiptoes	$3\frac{1}{2}$	25-30	50-60	1960-1989
ø1676/1	Tabitha Twitchett (blue striped 'V' neck)	$3\frac{1}{2}$	50-60	100-120	1960-1989
*1676/2	Tabitha Twitchett (white 'V' neck)	$3\frac{1}{2}$	35-40	70-80	1983-1989
*1796	Old Mr Brown	$3\frac{1}{4}$	35-40	70-80	1962-1989
1851	Anna Maria	3	120-140	240-300	1962-1982
1940/1	Mr Benjamin Bunny (left arm & pipe away from body)	$4\frac{1}{4}$	150-175	300-350	1964-1975
*1940/2	Mr Benjamin Bunny (left arm & pipe moulded into body)	$4\frac{1}{4}$	35-40	70-80	1975-1989
1941/1	Cecily Parsley (ears up and head down)	4	70-90	140-180	1964-1986
***1941/2	Cecily Parsley (ears back and head up)	4	30-35	60-70	1986-1989
*1942	Mrs Flopsy Bunny	4	35-50	70-80	1964-1989
2061	Amiable Guinea Pig	$3\frac{1}{2}$	150-200	300-400	1966-1982
***2276	Aunt Pettitoes	$3\frac{3}{4}$	40-45	80-90	1969-1989
***2284	Cousin Ribby	$3\frac{1}{4}$	40-45	80-90	1969-1989
*2333	Appley Dapply	$3\frac{1}{4}$	30-35	60-70	1970-1989
2334	Pickles	$4\frac{1}{2}$	150-175	300-350	1970-1982
2381	Pig-Wig	4	250-300	500-600	1971-1982
*2424	Mr Alderman Ptolemy	$3\frac{3}{4}$	65-75	130-150	1972-1989
2425	Sir Isaac Newton	$3\frac{7}{8}$	150-175	300-350	1972-1984
***2452	Sally Hennypenny	4	40-45	80-90	1973-1989
2453/1	Mr Jackson (green)	$2\frac{3}{4}$	150-200	300-400	1973-1982
*2453/2	Mr Jackson (fawn)	$2\frac{3}{4}$	40-45	80-90	1982-1989
2508	Simpkin	4	350-400	700-800	1974-1982
ø2509	Mr Benjamin Bunny & Peter Rabbit	4	60-75	120-150	1974-1989

*2543	Mrs Rabbit & Bunnies	3½	40-45	80-90	1975-1989
***2544	Tabitha Twitchett with Miss Moppett	3½	60-76	120-150	1975-1989
2559	Ginger	3¾	350-400	700-800	1976-1982
*2560	Poorly Peter Rabbit	3½	30-35	60-70	1976-1989
*2584	Hunca Munca Sweeping	3⅛	35-40	70-80	1977-1989
*2585	Little Black Rabbit	4⅜	35-40	70-80	1977-1989
2586/1	Fierce Bad Rabbit (feet up)	4¾	100-125	200-250	1977-1987
*2586/2	Fierce Bad Rabbit (feet down)	4¾	35-40	70-80	1987-1989
2601	The Duchess (see also 1355)	4	125-150	250-300	1977-1982
***2627	Chippy Hackee	3¾	25-30	50-60	1978-1989
*2628	Mr Drake Puddleduck	4¼	35-40	70-80	1978-1989
*2647	Rebeccah Puddleduck	3¼	35-40	70-80	1979-1989
****2668	Thomasina Tittlemouse	3¼	30-35	60-70	1980-1990
*2713	Diggory Diggory Delvet	2¾	40-50	80-100	1981-1989
****2716	Susan	4½	75-100	150-200	1981-1990
****2767	Old Mr Pricklepin	2½	35-40	70-80	1982-1990
2803/1	Benjamin Bunny Sat On A Bank (head to side)	3¾	35-40	70-80	1982-1987
*2803/2	Benjamin Bunny Sat On A Bank (head to front)	3¾	30-35	60-70	1987-1989
*2804	Old Woman Who Lived in a Shoe — knitting	3	100-125	200-250	1982-1989
*2823	Jemima Puddleduck Made A Feather Nest	2¼	30-35	60-70	1983-1989
*2877	Mrs Tiggy Winkle Takes Tea	3¼	100-125	200-250	1985-1989
*2878	Cottontail	3½	30-35	60-70	1985-1989
ø2956	Old Mr Bouncer	2⅞	30-35	60-70	1986-1989
*2957	Goody and Timmy Tiptoes	4	125-150	250-300	1986-1989
*2965	John Joiner (Dog)	2½	13.95	RRP	1990-C
*2966	Mother Ladybird	2½	13.95	RRP	1989-C
***2971	Babbitty Bumble (Bee)	2¾	25-30	50-60	1989-1993
*2989	Tom Thumb	3	75-95	150-200	1988-1989
*2996	Timmy Willie sleeping	1¾	90-110	180-225	1988-1989
**3030	Tom Kitten & Butterfly	3½	125-150	250-300	1988-1989
***3031	Little Pig Robinson spying	3½	150-175	300-350	1988-1989
**3090	Mr Jeremy Fisher digging	3½	150-175	300-350	1988-1989
***3091	Mr Tod	4¾	200-225	400-475	1988-1989
**3094	Johnny Townmouse with bag	3½	125-150	250-300	1988-1989
ø†3157	Peter In The Gooseberry Net	2	16.95	RRP	1990-1995
†3193	Jemima Puddleduck with Foxy Whiskered Gentleman	4¾	24·95	RRP	1990-C
†3197	Mittens & Moppet	3¾	20-25	40-50	1990-1994
†3200	Gentleman Mouse Made A Bow	3	13.95	RRP	1990-C
†3219	Foxy Reading Country News	4¼	21.00	RRP	1990-C
†3220	Lady Mouse Made A Curtsy	2¾	13·95	RRP	1990-C
†3234	Benjamin Wakes Up	2¼	13·95	RRP	1991-C
†3242	Peter And The Red Pocket Handkerchief	4½	15·95	RRP	1991-C
†ø3251	Miss Dormouse	4	19·95	RRP	1991-1995
†3252	Pigling Eats His Porridge	4	20-25	40-50	1991-1994
†3257	Christmas Stocking (Hunca Munca & Wife)	3½	25-30	50-60	1991-1994
†3278	Mrs Rabbit Cooking	4	13·95	RRP	1992-C

†3280	Ribby & the Patty Pan	$3\frac{1}{2}$	13·95	RRP	1992-C
†3288	Hunca Munca Spills the Beads	$3\frac{1}{4}$	15·95	RRP	1992-C
†3317	Benjamin Bunny Eats A Lettuce Leaf	$4\frac{3}{4}$	13.95	RRP	1992-C
†3319	And This Little Pig Had None	$3\frac{1}{2}$	13.95	RRP	1992-C
†3325	No More Twist	$3\frac{5}{8}$	13.95	RRP	1992-C
††3356	Peter Rabbit (large size)	$6\frac{3}{4}$	26.95	RRP	1993-C
†3372	Jeremy Fisher (large size)	5	26.95	RRP	1994-C
†††3373	Jemima Puddleduck (large size)	$6\frac{1}{4}$	26.95	RRP	1994-C
†3398	Mrs Rabbit (large size)	6	26.95	RRP	1994-C
†3403	Benjamin Bunny (large size)	6	26.95	RRP	1994-C
†3405	Tom Kitten (large size)	$5\frac{1}{4}$	26.95	RRP	1994-C
†3449	The Tailor of Gloucester (large size)	$7\frac{1}{4}$	26.95	RRP	1995-C
†3450	Fox Whiskered Gentleman (large size)	7	26.95	RRP	1995-C
†3473	Peter in Bed	$2\frac{3}{4}$	18.50	RRP	1995-C

Beatrix Potter – Wall Plaques, stand and Tree lamp base

1531	Tree lamp base	7	65-75	130-150	1958-1982
2082	Jemima Puddleduck (plaque)	6	750-1000	1500-2000	1966-1969
2083	Peter Rabbit (plaque)	6	750-1000	1500-2000	1966-1969
2085	Tom Kitten (plaque)	6	750-1000	1500-2000	1966-1969
*2295	Display Stand	$12\frac{1}{2} \times 2\frac{1}{2}$	20-25	40-50	1969-1989
2594	Jemima Puddleduck & Foxy Whiskered Gentleman (plaque)	$7\frac{1}{2} \times 7\frac{1}{2}$	80-100	175-225	1977-1982
2650	Peter Rabbit (plaque)	$7\frac{1}{2} \times 7\frac{1}{2}$	75-85	150-175	1979-1983
2685	Mrs Tittlemouse (plaque)	$7\frac{1}{2} \times 7\frac{1}{2}$	100-110	200-225	1981-1984

Beatrix Potter – Character Jugs

****2959	Old Mr Brown	$2\frac{1}{2}$	40-50	80-100	1987-1992
****2960	Jeremy Fisher	$2\frac{3}{4}$	40-50	80-100	1987-1992
****3006	Peter Rabbit	$2\frac{3}{4}$	40-50	80-100	1988-1992
****3088	Jemima Puddleduck	$3\frac{1}{4}$	50-60	100-125	1988-1992
****3102	Mrs Tigglewinkle	3	50-60	100-125	1988-1992
****3103	Tom Kitten	3	50-60	100-125	1988-1992

Beatrix Potter boxed sets

These sets consist of a transparent window box containing a copy of one of the 'little books' by Beatrix Potter, together with the relevant model. All were available with either Beswick or Royal Albert backstamps

Model No	Name of Book and Model	Current Value Beswick £/$	R Albert £/$	Production Period
1092/2	Jemima Puddleduck	45/RRP	20/RRP	1/86-C
1098/2	Peter Rabbit	45/RRP	20/RRP	1/86-C
1100	Tom Kitten	45/90	20/40	8/87-12/92
1101	Timmy Tiptoes	35/70	20/40	8/88-12/92
1102	Squirrel Nutkin	35/70	20/40	1/90-12/92
1103	Mrs Tittlemouse	35/70	20/40	8/88-12/92

1105/3	Benjamin Bunny	40/RRP	20/RRP	1/86-C
1106	Samuel Whiskers	40/80	20/40	1/90-12/92
1107/2	Mrs Tiggy Winkle	40/RRP	20/RRP	1/86-C
1108	Tailor of Gloucester	35/70	20/40	8/87-12/92
1157	Jeremy Fisher	35/70	20/40	8/87-12/92
1275	Miss Moppet	40/80	20/40	8/88-12/92
1276	Johnny Townmouse	35/70	20/40	1/90-12/92
2333	Appley Dapply	35/70	20/RRP	8/87-12/92
2586/1	Fierce Bad Rabbit	115/225	n/a	8/88-12/92
2586/2	Fierce Bad Rabbit	45/90	20/40	8/88-12/92

Model No	Name of Model	Height inches	Current Value £	$	Production Period

Snow White and the Seven Dwarfs Figures

Model No	Name of Model	Height inches	£	$	Production Period
1325	Dopey	$3\frac{1}{2}$	100-150	200-300	1954-1967
1326	Happy	$3\frac{1}{2}$	100-150	200-300	1954-1967
1327	Bashful	$3\frac{1}{2}$	100-150	200-300	1954-1967
1328	Sneezy	$3\frac{1}{2}$	100-150	200-300	1954-1967
1329	Doc	$3\frac{1}{2}$	100-150	200-300	1954-1967
1330	Grumpy	$3\frac{1}{2}$	100-150	200-300	1954-1967
1331	Sleepy	$3\frac{1}{2}$	100-150	200-300	1954-1967
1332	Snow White	5	300-350	600-700	1954-1967

Winnie the Pooh Figures

Model No	Name of Model	Height inches	£	$	Production Period
2193	Winnie the Pooh	$2\frac{1}{2}$	40-45	80-90	1968-1990
2196	Eeyore	2	35-40	70-80	1968-1990
2214	Piglet	$2\frac{3}{4}$	50-60	100-120	1968-1990
2215	Rabbit	$3\frac{1}{8}$	35-40	70-80	1968-1990
2216	Owl	3	30-35	60-70	1968-1990
2217	Kanga	$3\frac{1}{8}$	30-35	60-70	1968-1990
2394	Tigger	3	65-75	130-150	1971-1990
2395	Christopher Robin	$4\frac{3}{4}$	90-100	180-200	1971-1990

Alice in Wonderland Figures

Model No	Name of Model	Height inches	£	$	Production Period
2476	Alice	$4\frac{3}{4}$	175-225	350-450	1973-1983
2477	White Rabbit	$4\frac{3}{4}$	175-225	350-450	1973-1983
2478	Mock Turtle	$4\frac{1}{4}$	60-80	120-160	1973-1983
2479	Mad Hatter	$4\frac{1}{4}$	125-175	250-350	1973-1983
2480	Cheshire Cat	$1\frac{1}{2}$	350-400	700-800	1973-1983
2485	Gryphon	$3\frac{1}{4}$	50-75	100-150	1973-1983
2489	King of Hearts	$3\frac{3}{4}$	50-60	100-120	1973-1983
2490	Queen of Hearts	4	50-60	100-120	1973-1983
2545	Dodo	4	100-125	200-250	1975-1983
2546	Fish Footman	$4\frac{5}{8}$	125-175	250-350	1975-1983
2547	Frog Footman	$4\frac{1}{4}$	150-200	300-400	1975-1983

Kitty MacBride Figures

Model No	Name of Model	Height inches	£	$	Production Period
2526	A Family Mouse	$3\frac{3}{8}$	30-40	60-80	1975-1983
2527	A Double Act	$3\frac{3}{8}$	30-40	60-80	1975-1983
2528	The Racegoer	$3\frac{3}{8}$	30-40	60-80	1975-1983
2529	A Good Read	$2\frac{5}{8}$	175-225	350-450	1975-1983
2530	Lazy Bones	$1\frac{5}{8}$	30-40	60-80	1975-1983
2531	A Snack	$3\frac{1}{4}$	30-40	60-80	1975-1983
2532	Strained Relations	$3\frac{1}{8}$	30-40	30-40	1975-1983
2533	Just Good Friends	$3\frac{1}{8}$	40-50	80-100	1975-1983

2565	The Ring	3¼	50-75	100-150	1976-1983
2566	Guilty Sweethearts	2¼	40-50	80-100	1976-1983
2589	All I Do Is Think of You	2⅜	80-100	160-200	1977-1983

Walt Disney Character Figures

1278	Mickey Mouse	3⅞	300-400	600-800	1952-1965
1279	Jiminy Cricket	4	300-400	600-800	1952-1965
1280	Pluto	3½	300-400	600-800	1953-1965
1281	Goofy	4¼	300-400	600-800	1953-1965
1282	Pinocchio	4	300-400	600-800	1953-1965
1283	Donald Duck	4	300-400	600-800	1953-1965
1289	Minnie Mouse	4	300-400	600-800	1953-1965
1291	Thumper	3¾	300-400	600-800	1953-1965
1301	Nana	3¼	300-400	600-800	1953-1965
1302	Smee	4⅛	300-400	600-800	1953-1965
1307	Peter Pan	5	300-400	600-800	1953-1965
1312	Tinkerbell	5	300-400	600-800	1953-1965

Rupert Bear Figures

2694	Rupert Bear	4¼	180-220	360-450	1980-1986
2710	Algy Pug	4	60-80	120-160	1981-1986
2711	Pong Ping	4¼	60-80	120-160	1981-1986
2720	Bill Badger	2¾	80-100	160-200	1981-1986
2779	Rupert Bear snowballing	4¼	200-250	400-500	1982-1986

Wind in the Willows Figures

†2939	Mole — AW4	3	20-25	40-50	1987-1989
†2940	Badger — AW3	3	20-25	40-50	1987-1989
†2941	Ratty— AW2	3⅝	20-25	40-50	1987-1989
†2942	Toad — AW1	3⅝	20-25	40-50	1987-1989
†3065	Portly (Otter) AW6	2¾	80-100	160-200	1988-1989
†3076	Weasel Gamekeeper AW5	4	80-100	160-200	1988-1989

Thelwell Figures

2704	An Angel on Horseback	4½	60-80	120-160	1981-1989
2769	Kick Start	3½	60-80	120-160	1982-1989
2789	Pony Express	4½	60-80	120-160	1982-1989

All three available in Bay and Grey

David Hand Animal Land Figures

1148	Dinkum Platypus	4¼	150-200	300-400	1949-1955
1150	Zimmy Lion	3¾	300-350	600-700	1949-1955
1151	Felia Cat	4	300-350	600-700	1949-1955
1152	Ginger Nutt	4	150-200	300-400	1949-1955
1153	Hazel Nutt	3¾	150-200	300-400	1949-1955
1154	Oscar Ostrich	3¾	300-350	600-700	1949-1955
1155	Dusty Mole	3½	150-200	300-400	1949-1955
1156	Loopy Hare	4¼	300-350	600-700	1949-1955

Remainder not in categories

857	Alice & White Rabbit (on base)	—	75-90	150-180	1940-1950
858	Dormouse &Alice (plaque)	—	75-90	150-180	1940-1950

859	King & Alice (plaque)	—	75-90	150-180	1940-1950
860	Alice playing croquet (on base)	—	75-90	150-180	1940-1950
861	Cinderella feeding birds (plaque)	—	75-90	150-180	1940-1950
863	Cinderella dressing the ugly sisters (plaque)	—	75-90	150-180	1940-1950
865	Cinderella running from the ball (plaque)	—	75-90	150-180	1940-1950
866	Cinderella & slipper (plaque)	—	75-90	150-180	1940-1950
867	The Prince finds Cinderella (plaque)	—	75-90	150-180	1940-1950

*Still currently available with a Royal Albert backstamp
**Available with a Royal Albert backstamp 1989-1994
***Available with a Royal Albert backstamp 1989-1993
****Small number available with a Royal Albert backstamp
øAvailable with a Royal Albert backstamp 1989-1995
†Only available with Royal Albert backstamp
††Beswick backstamp 1993 only, then Royal Albert
†††Beswick backstamp 1994 only, then Royal Albert

2779 Rupert snowballing. The hardest one to find

Comical Animals and Birds

(All models carry a Beswick backstamp)

Apart from their modelling skills many of the Beswick artists have had another strong asset, a lively sense of humour, and this is reflected in a large number of pieces in the collection. A time-honoured way of raising a smile is to endow an animal with human characteristics, and so it is not surprising to find dogs, cats and monkeys playing musical instruments, a cat hiking, a duck on skis, penguins sporting umbrellas and even a monkey smoking a pipe, one of the most appealing studies in the group. Sometimes facial expressions alone are sufficient to amuse, as with the dog going cross-eyed looking at a ladybird on the end of his nose (804). Occasionally the animals themselves join in the joke — there are laughing pigs, cats and a dog introduced in 1967.

Frequently the Beswick artists have sought comedy in familiar situations such as the cats curled up on chimney pots which form a cruet set in the 'Fun Ceramics' collection or the snoozing pigs in the 'Farmyard Humour' series.

More recently the 'Little Loveable' Clown Series has been introduced, together with the 'English Country Folk' and 'Pig Prom' series. These are listed separately later in the book.

The ability to entertain in this way is an endearing aspect of the Beswick story and hopefully the laughter will continue for many years to come.

Model No	Name of Model	Height inches	Current Value £	$	Production Period
317	Duck on base	8¼	75-100	150-200	1936-1954
324	Poodle begging	7	75-100	150-200	1936-1954
624	Rabbit with knapsack	4	50-60	100-120	1938-1954
663	Elephant with five ton weight (spill holder)	—	45-50	90-100	1938-1954
664	Fox with elbow on tree trunk (spill holder)	4½	50-60	100-120	1938-1954
665	Rabbit with golf bag (spill holder)	4¾	50-60	100-120	1938-1954
688	Teddy bear	—	50-75	100-150	1939-1954
697	Hippo Laughing	2¼	45-50	90-100	1939-1954
698/1	Giraffe (large)	—	50-60	100-120	1939-1954
698/2	Giraffe (medium)	—	45-55	90-110	1939-1954
698/3	Giraffe (small)	—	40-50	80-100	1940-1954
760	Duck with ladybird on nose	3⅞	15-20	30-40	1939-1971
761	Dog with bandage	4¼	35-45	70-90	1939-1971
762	Duck on skis	3¼	25-35	50-70	1939-1969
765	Three Ducks	2¾	20-25	40-50	1939-1971
802	Penguin with umbrella up	4¼	25-30	50-60	1940-1972
803	Penguin with walking stick (Part of set see 800 and 801 in Birds)	3¾	20-25	50-60	1940-1972
804	Dog with ladybird on nose	4	15-20	30-40	1940-1969
805/1	Dog with ladybird on tail	3¾	15-20	30-40	1940-1969
805/2	Dog with ladybird on tail	2½	10-15	20-30	1940-1969
811	Dog playing accordian	4	45-50	90-100	1940-1961
812	Dog asleep on drum	2⅞	35-40	70-80	1940-1961
813	Dog with ladybird on nose	4	15-20	30-40	1940-1967
831	Dog with glasses reading book	6¼	75-100	150-200	1940-1961
907	Dog with ladybird on tail	3¼	10-15	20-30	1941-1971

1001	Cockerel	5¾	100-125	200-250	1944-1961
1002	Puppit dog	4¾	35-45	70-90	1944-1969
1003	Fawnie	5¼	75-95	150-200	1944-1967
1004	Rooster	7	100-125	200-250	1944-1961
1005	Kangarinie	5	100-125	200-250	1944-1961
1006	Grebie (small duck)	5¼	100-125	200-250	1944-1954
1026	Cat orchestra conductor	2	20-25	40-50	1945-1972
1027	Cat cellist	2	20-25	40-50	1945-1972
1028	Cat violinist	2	20-25	40-50	1945-1972
1029	Cat saxophonist	2	20-25	40-50	1945-1972
1049	Monkey smoking pipe	4¼	50-60	100-120	1946-1968
1054	Dog holding 'My Plate'	4¼	40-50	80-90	1947-1967
1058	Dog	4½	35-45	70-90	1946-1967
1088	Dog	3½	30-40	60-80	1947-1968
1255	Monkey drummer	2⅝	100-125	200-250	1952-1962
1256	Monkey tuba player	2⅝	100-125	200-250	1952-1962
1257	Monkey fiddler	2⅝	100-125	200-250	1952-1962
1258	Monkey saxophonist	2⅝	100-125	200-250	1952-1962
1259	Monkey guitarist	2⅝	100-125	200-250	1952-1962
1260	Monkey banjo player	2⅝	100-125	200-250	1952-1962
1335	Tortoise mother	2¾ long	50-60	100-120	1954-1972
1336	Tortoise girl	1¾ long	25-35	50-70	1954-1972
1337	Tortoise boy	1¾ long	25-35	50-70	1954-1972
1379	Bush Baby with mirror	2	40-50	80-100	1955-1965
1380	Bush Baby with stud	2	40-50	80-100	1955-1965
1381	Bush Baby with candy	1½	40-50	80-100	1955-1965
1733	Fox	3¾	50-60	100-120	1962-1968
1738	Pup with bone	3¾	60-75	120-150	1962-1967
2100	Cat and mouse laughing	3	50-60	100-120	1967-1972
2101	Cat laughing	3	40-50	80-100	1967-1972

*Pig and Piglet **2746** and Daisy the Cow **2792**, both in the Comical series*

2102	Dog laughing	$2\frac{7}{8}$	40-50	80-100	1967-1972
2103	Two Pigs laughing	$2\frac{3}{4}$	50-60	100-120	1967-1971
2130	Dog praying	$2\frac{7}{8}$	40-50	80-100	1967-1972
2131	Rabbit yawning	$2\frac{7}{8}$	40-50	80-100	1967-1972
2132	Rabbit & baby asleep	$2\frac{7}{8}$	60-80	120-160	1967-1971
2200	Chicken running	$1\frac{1}{4}$	25-30	50-60	1968-1973
2201	Chicken pecking	1	25-30	50-60	1968-1973
2202	Chicken sitting	$1\frac{1}{2}$	25-30	50-60	1968-1973
2746	Pig & piglet riding piggy back	$2\frac{3}{4}$	20-25	40-50	1981-1994
2761	Cat asleep on chimney. Salt, pepper and stand	4	40-60	80-120	1982-1986
2792	Daisy the Cow creamer	$5\frac{3}{4}$	30-40	60-80	1983-1989
2802	Umbrella money box "Saving for a Rainy Day"	$5\frac{1}{4}$	35-40	70-80	1983-1986
2805	Pillar Box money box with cat on top	$6\frac{1}{4}$	35-40	70-80	1983-1986
2810	Egg cup with cat	$2\frac{3}{8}$	20-25	40-50	1983-1986
*3012	Sporting Cat Footballer in striped colours	$4\frac{1}{8}$	25-35	50-70	1987 only
A	Orange and White				
B	Maroon and White				
C	Black and White				
D	Light Blue and White				
E	Yellow & White				
*3016	Sporting Cat Footballer in plain colours	$4\frac{1}{8}$	25-35	50-70	1987 only
A	Orange and White				
B	Maroon and White				
C	Black and White				
D	Light Blue and White				
E	Yellow & White				
*3023	Sporting Cat Cricketer	$4\frac{1}{8}$			
*3027	Sporting Cat Bowls	$4\frac{1}{8}$			
*3039	Sporting Cat Tennis	$4\frac{1}{8}$			

In this projected series, only the Footballer Cats were put into very limited production and are now scarce.

English Country Folk

(All models carry a Beswick backstamp)

These very collectable, gloss finish, humorous animal characters were introduced in September 1993, with further additions in mid 1994. Portraying animals dressed as humans, they herald the start of a new collection, with close attention to detail.

Each one carries its own 'ECF' number and these are listed below.

Model No	*Name of Model*	*ECF No*	*Height inches*	*Current Value £*	*$*	*Production Period*
3417	Gentleman Pig	4	5¾	22.50	RRP	1993-C
3418	Huntsman Fox	1	5¾	22.50	RRP	1993-C
3419	Fisherman Otter	2	5¾	22.50	RRP	1993-C
3420	Gardener Rabbit	3	6	22.50	RRP	1993-C
3421	Hiker Badger	6	5¼	22.50	RRP	1993-C
3422	Shepherd Sheepdog	5	6¾	22.50	RRP	1993-C
3447	Mrs Rabbit Baking	7	5½	22.50	RRP	1994-C
3448	Lady Pig	8	5½	22.50	RRP	1994-C

Pig Prom Musicians

(Special backstamp for 1994 only)

This superb set of gloss finish humorous pig musicians, each playing a different musical instrument, was introduced in 1994. For this introductory year only, the early 'Beswick Ware' backstamp will be used, thereafter, the plain 'Beswick England' backstamp will appear.

It is interesting to note that each pig is of a different breed. Each one carries its own 'PP' number and these are listed below.

Model No	*Name of Model*	*PP No*	*Height inches*	*Current Value £*	*$*	*Production Period*
3440	Andrew — Cymbal Player Gloucester Old Spot	4	4¾	22.50	RRP	1994-C
3443	Mathew— Trumpet Player Large White	2	6	22.50	RRP	1994-C
3444	David — Flute Player Tamworth	3	5¼	22.50	RRP	1994-C
3446	John — Conductor Vietnamese Pot-Bellied	1	4⅝	22.50	RRP	1994-C
3453	Daniel — Violin Player Saddleback	5	5¼	22.50	RRP	1994-C
3454	Michael — Bass Drum Player — Large Black	6	4¾	22.50	RRP	1994-C

Figures

(All models carry a Beswick backstamp)

Beswick have produced a wide variety of figures. From 1894 they made the traditional Staffordshire types and continued production of these long after other manufacturers had ceased.

The first figure recorded in the existing pattern books was a smiling policeman directing traffic (303). This is an isolated model as the majority of the figures in the 1930s and 40s portrayed children, mostly modelled by Miss Greaves.

During World War Two Beswick introduced their Kindergarten series, copies of the popular Hummel style figures made in Germany by Goebbels. Beswick exported most of these pieces to America and Canada but, after the war, when Germany was again able to export, Beswick ceased production. As they were produced only throughout the war years, these pieces are now very rare. The original Hummel model number for each figure is recorded in the lists.

This cute style of figure was revived briefly in 1969 when Arthur Hallam modelled a series of doll-like children based upon drawings in a book by Joan Welsh Anglund, entitled, *A Friend Is Someone Who Loves You*, first published in 1959.

In the opinion of many collectors the finest Beswick figures are those designed by Miss Granoska between 1951 and 1954. Most portray characters in national costume, often accompanied by animals. One set depicts obstinate donkeys and goats carrying panniers of apples and grapes, being led, pushed or ridden by European peasants, whilst another group features national dancers of the world.

During the 1950s a number of figures appeared on horse-back, ranging from Colin Melbourne's stylised clowns riding bare-back to more realistic portraits of huntsmen and soldiers in the saddle. The latter are classed under the horses group.

Beswick have also produced many figures inspired by characters from film and literature and these are listed in their appropriate section.

Model No	Name of Model	Height inches	Current Value £	$	Production Period
303	Policeman (on base)	—	150-200	300-400	1935-1954
374	Girl tasting honey (on base)	5	150-200	300-400	1936-1954
375	Boy (on base)	—	150-200	300-400	1936-1954
388	Girl — finger in mouth	5¾	150-200	300-400	1936-1954
389	Man on rock	—	150-200	300-400	1936-1954
390	Girl in breeze (on base)	5½	150-200	300-400	1936-1954
391	Girl with hands in muff	7¼	150-200	300-400	1936-1954
437	Girl with flared dress	4¾	150-200	300-400	1936-1954
438	Girl with frilled dress	—	150-200	300-400	1936-1954
441	Lady standing on base	—	150-200	300-400	1936-1954
442	Man standing on base	—	150-200	300-400	1936-1954
443	Child sitting	—	150-200	300-400	1936-1954
501	Clown	—	150-200	300-400	1937-1954

622	Mr Chamberlain	—	100-125	200-250	1938-1940
751	Boy Soldier facing left in front of sentry box (bookend)	6	100-125	200-250	1939-1954
751	Boy Soldier facing right in front of sentry box (bookend)	6	100-125	200-250	1939-1954
903	Bugle Boy (Hummel 97)	6	250-300	500-600	1940-1948
904	Book Worm (Hummel 3)	5	250-300	500-600	1940-1948
905	Goose Girl (Hummel 47)	6¼	250-300	500-600	1940-1948
906	Strolling Along (Hummel 5)	4¾	250-300	500-600	1941-1948
908	Stormy Weather (Hummel 71)	6	250-300	500-600	1941-1948
909	Puppy Love (Hummel 1)	5¼	250-300	500-600	1941-1948
910	Meditation (Hummel 13)	5	250-300	500-600	1941-1948
911	Max & Moritz (Hummel 123)	5¾	250-300	500-600	1941-1948
912	Farm Boy (Hummel 66)	6	250-300	500-600	1941-1948
913	Globe Trotter (Hummel 109)	5	250-300	500-600	1941-1948
914	Shepherd's Boy (Hummel 64)	4¼	250-300	500-600	1941-1948
924	Winston Churchill waving hat	6	200-250	400-500	1941-1954
940	A.R.P Warden outside air raid shelter on one side, boy, girl and mother looking out on the other	—	100-125	200-250	1941-1946
952	Army Co-operation. Couple embracing on one side, soldier pulling pin from hand grenade on other	—	100-125	200-250	1941-1946
†990	Boy strumming banjo (Hummel)	3	500-600	1000-1200	1942only
1010	Fairy Crying	6	200-250	400-500	1944-1954
1011	Fairy Drinking	4	200-250	400-500	1944-1954
1012	Fairy Sewing	4¾	200-250	400-500	1944-1954
1013	Fairy Baking	—	200-250	400-500	1944-1954
1020	Madonna	14	200-250	400-500	1945-1954
1086	Clown & Dog on base	7¼	150-200	300-400	1947-1958
1087	Jester sitting	—	150-200	300-400	1947-1958
1091	Gypsy Girl	7¼	150-200	300-400	1947-1958
1093	Hiker Boy	6	150-200	300-400	1947-1954
1094	Hiker Girl	6	150-200	300-400	1947-1954
1096	Sportsman & Dog	6¾	150-200	300-400	1947-1958
1097	Fruit Seller (Pedlar)	—	150-200	300-400	1947-1958
1122	Butcher Boy with basket	5¾	150-200	300-400	1948-1958
1123	Man with flower pot	6¼	150-200	300-400	1948-1954
1124	Shepherd Boy with two sheep under arm	6¼	150-200	300-400	1948-1959
1125	Scotsman in kilt	6¼	150-200	300-400	1948-1954
1221	Hungarian Girl with turkey	7¼	150-200	300-400	1951-1962
1222	Polish Girl with hen	7	150-200	300-400	1951-1962
1223	Spaniard pulling donkey with panniers of apples	4½	150-200	300-400	1951-1962
1224	Spaniard pushing donkey with panniers of grapes	4½	150-200	300-400	1951-1962
1227	Swedish Girl holding cockerel	7	150-200	300-400	1952-1962
1230	Danish Girl leading pig	5¾	150-200	300-400	1952-1962
1234	Italian Girl leading goat	5½	150-200	300-400	1952-1962
1238	Italian Girl with goat eating hat	6	150-200	300-400	1952-1962
1244	Lady on donkey	5½	150-200	300-400	1952-1962

1245	Two children on donkey	4½	150-200	300-400	1952-1962
1247	Finnish Girl with duck	7	150-200	300-400	1952-1962
1262	Balinese Girl	3½	100-125	200-250	1952-1962
1263	Indian Girl	3½	100-125	200-250	1952-1962
1320	Siamese Dancer	3½	100-125	200-250	1953-1962
1321	Japanese Dancer	3½	100-125	200-250	1953-1962
1333	Chinese Dancer	3½	100-125	200-250	1954-1962
1334	Hawaiian Dancer	3½	100-125	200-250	1954-1962
1347	Susie Jamaica	7	150-175	300-350	1954-1975
1470	Clown on Horse (small) (CM series)	5¾	125-150	250-300	1957-1963
1476	Clown on horse (large) (CM series)	8½	150-200	300-400	1957-1963
1626	Toy drummer ⎫ coloured	2⅜	40-50	80-100	1959-1966
1627	Toy buglers ⎬ red and	2⅜	40-50	80-100	1959-1966
1628	Toy guards ⎭ blue	2⅜	40-50	80-100	1959-1966
1737	Man & Woman	8⅜	150-200	300-400	1961-1963
1766	Road Gang: Foreman	—	40-50	80-100	1961-1963
1767	Road Gang: Digger	—	40-50	80-100	1961-1963
1768	Road Gang: Driller	—	40-50	80-100	1961-1963
1769	Road Gang: At Ease	—	40-50	80-100	1961-1963
1801/2	Pianist & Piano	3	75-100 each	150-200	1963-1969
	See also 1803 in Cats Section		50-60	100-120	
1804	Boy without spectacles	3⅝	75-100	150-200	1963-1969
1805	Boy with spectacles	3	75-100	150-200	1963-1969
	See also 1824 in Dogs Section				
1825	Boy with guitar	3	75-100	150-200	1963-1969
1826	Girl with harp	3⅝	75-100	150-200	1963-1969
1878	Welsh Lady	5	50-60	100-125	1963-1969
1937	Bust of Lady (C.M.C. on base)	6	50-60	100-125	1964-1965
1993	Lady with fan	7½	150-200	300-400	1964-1965
1994	Lady with hat	7½	150-200	300-400	1964-1965
1995	Lady in ball gown	7	150-200	300-400	1964-1965
2181	Knight of St John	6¾	200-250	400-500	1968-1969
2272	Anglund Boy	4⅜	100-125	200-250	1969-1971
2293	Anglund Girl	4⅜	100-125	200-250	1969-1971
2317	Anglund Girl	4¾	100-125	200-250	1969-1971

†Not put into production

Little Loveables

This colourful series of ten different clowns were modelled by Amanda Hughes-Lubeck (8) and Warren Platt (2) in the John Beswick Studio, at Longton, under the watchful eye of Graham Tongue.

They first appeared at the end of 1992 and were notable in having suitable names printed on top of the base. Very shortly after their introduction, the name on model nos LL3, 10 and 17 — 'God Loves Me' was changed to 'Please' and this has naturally meant that the short supply of 'God Loves Me' has put a premium on this particular one.

The other interesting fact is that LL15-LL21 were Parian versions for the American market. Each model is available in two different colour combinations (with a gloss finish) and a third Parian version which has a matt finish. There is also a set without any names on the base.

Full details of the separate LL numbers together with the Beswick model numbers are given in the list which follows:

LL No	Model No	Model Name	Gloss or Matt	Colour of Stripes	Colour of Spots	Size	Current Value £	$	Production Period
1	3328	Happy Birthday	G	Pale Pink	Bright Orange	4½	15-20	30-40	1992-1994
2	3320	I Love You	G	Light Green	Pale Pink	4½	15-20	30-40	1992-1994
*3	3336	God Loves Me	G	Light Green	Turquoise	3¾	25-30	50-60	1992-1993
4	3361	Just For You	G	Pale Pink	Turquoise	4½	15-20	30-40	1992-1994
5	3331	To Mother	G	Turquoise	Purple	4½	15-20	30-40	1992-1994
6	3340	Congratulations	G	Dark Green	Pale Pink	4½	15-20	30-40	1992-1994
7	3334	Passed	G	Lilac	Pale Pink	3	15-20	30-40	1992-1994
8	3328	Happy Birthday	G	Orange/Yellow	Dark Green	4½	15-20	30-40	1992-1994
9	3320	I Love You	G	Lilac	Orange/Yellow	4½	15-20	30-40	1992-1994
*10	3336	God Loves Me	G	Orange/Yellow	Powder Blue	3¾	25-30	50-80	1992-1993
11	3361	Just For You	G	Orange/Yellow	Mint Green	4½	15-20	30-40	1992-1994
12	3331	To Mother	G	Peach/Yellow	Pale Pink	4½	15-20	30-40	1992-1994
13	3340	Congratulations	G	Turquoise	Orange/Yellow	4½	15-20	30-40	1992-1994
14	3334	Passed	G	Pale Blue	Bright Orange	3	15-20	30-40	1992-1994
15	3407	Happy Birthday	M	Coral	Leaf Green	4½	20-25	40-50	1992-1993
16	3406	I Love You	M	Dover Green	Pale Yellow	4½	20-25	40-50	1992-1993
**17	3410	God Loves Me	M	Crimson	Pale Yellow	3¾	30-35	60-70	1992-1993
18	3412	Just For You	M	Bright Yellow	Bright Blue	4½	20-25	40-50	1992-1993
19	3408	To Mother	M	Leaf Green	Orange	4½	20-25	40-50	1992-1993
20	3411	Congratulations	M	Bright Blue	Bright Red	4½	20-25	40-50	1992-1993
21	3409	Passed	M	Bright Blue	Orange	3	20-25	40-50	1992-1993
22	3328	No Name Sandy coloured base	G	Pale Pink	Bright Orange	4½	20-25	40-50	1993 only
23	3320	No Name Sandy coloured base	G	Light Green	Pale Pink	4½	20-25	40-50	1993 only
24	3336	No Name Sandy coloured base	G	Light Green	Turquoise	3¾	20-25	40-50	1993 only
25	3361	No Name Sandy coloured base	G	Pale Pink	Turquoise Blue	4½	20-25	40-50	1993 only
26	3331	No Name Sandy coloured base	G	Turquoise	Purple	4¼	20-25	40-50	1993 only
27	3340	No Name Sandy coloured base	G	Dark Green	Pale Pink	4½	20-25	40-50	1993 only
28	3334	No Name Sandy coloured base	G	Lilac	Pale Pink	3	20-25	40-50	1993 only
29	3331	To Daddy	G	Turquoise	Mint Green	4½	25-30	50-60	1994 only
30	3389	Merry Christmas	G	Bright Red	Dark Green & toys	4	25-30	50-60	1993-1994
31	3388	Good Luck	G	Pale Pink	Mint Green	4¼	25-30	50-60	1993-1994

32	3390	Get Well Soon	G	Dark Green	Vivid Purple	4¼	25-30	50-60	1994 only
33	3336	Please	G	Light Green	Turquoise	3¾	15-20	30-40	1993-1994
34	3336	Please	G	Orange/ Yellow	Powder Blue	3¾	15-20	30-40	1993-1994
***35	3320	I Love Beswick	G	'Beswick' Green	Yellow	4½			1995 only

*Name changed to 'Please' and transferred to LL33 and LL34
**Name changed to 'Please' 4/93.
***Beswick Collectors Circle special model

Thunderbirds

(All carry the Beswick backstamp)

To celebrate the 30th anniversary of this popular TV childrens programme, Lawleys By Post commissioned the John Beswick Studio of Royal Doulton to create a collection of six 4" high busts of the most popular characters from the series. Modelled by William K Harper in 1992 as a numbered edition of 2,500 they were only available, by post, in a set of six, at a price of £237.

It is believed that, possibly, only about 500 sets were actually produced and sold as a numbered set. This would make the series very collectable in the future.

Model No	Name of Model	Current value		Production
		£	$	Period
3337	Lady Penelope	45-50	90-100	1992-1993
3339	Brains	45-50	90-100	1992-1993
3344	Scott Tracy	45-50	90-100	1992-1993
3345	Virgil Tracy	45-50	90-100	1992-1993
3346	Parker	45-50	90-100	1992-1993
3348	The Hood	45-50	90-100	1992-1993

Little Likeables

(All models carry a John Beswick backstamp)

This collection of bone china animals, sculptures from the John Beswick Studio of Royal Doulton, broke new ground when they were first announced in the January 1985 price list.

All white, with a minimum of gold and pastel colouring and with a gloss finish, they immediately set new standards for the Beswick animal studies and had an irresistable charm of their own.

They were never illustrated in any form of catalogue, other than trade issues and so very little is known about them.

The series is very collectable and extremely well modelled by Robert Tabbenor and Diane Griffiths and should be on the 'shopping list' of every dedicated Beswick collector.

By the end of 1986 they were beginning to be difficult to find and when the January 1987 price list was issued, the reason became clear, they had been withdrawn!

Each model was individually priced in an attractive gift box and prices ranged betweed £10 and £15. The following collectors list gives all the information known about each model.

Model No	Name of Model	Height inches	Modeller	Current Value £	$
LL1	'Family gathering' (Hen and 2 chicks)	4½	Diane Griffiths	20-25	40-50
LL2	'Watching The World Go By' (Frog)	3¾	Robert Tabbenor	25-30	50-80
LL3	'Hide and Sleep' (Pig and 2 piglets)	3¼	Robert Tabbenor	20-25	40-50
LL4	'My Pony' (Pony)	7¼	Diane Griffiths	25-30	50-80
LL5	'On Top Of The World' (Elephant)	3¾	Diane Grffiths	20-25	40-50
LL6	'Treat Me Gently' (Fawn)	4½	Diane Griffiths	20-25	40-50
LL7	'Out At Last' (Duckling)	3¼	Robert Tabbenor	20-25	40-50
LL8	'Cats Chorus'	4¾	Robert Tabbenor	20-25	40-50

Studio Sculptures

This range of animal and bird studies was created by Design Manager Harry Sales and introduced in January 1985.

A new bonded ceramic body was used, which has the ability of capturing all the minute detail of each subject and literally brings it to life in a three-dimensional re-creation of the original drawing.

The initial sculpture entails a great deal of intricate modelling to achieve this and it is the final hand decoration on the finished product which really brings each sculpture to life.

Each item was separately boxed in specially designed packaging and some were available on polished hardwood bases.

The series is now discontinued and individual pieces will therefore be very hard to find.

The shortest production runs were of model numbers 26 to 30 (inclusive) which were only available for six months.

A green baize is applied to the whole of the base on each model and an adhesive label is then applied on top of this, giving model details.

It should be noted that model numbers 23 to 25 (inclusive) were not produced.

Model No	Name of Model	Size inches	Current Value £	$	Production Period
BEATRIX POTTER SERIES					
SS1	Timmy Willie	4¼	30-40	60-80	1/85-12/85
*SS2	Flopsy Bunnies	5	50-75	100-150	1/85-12/85
*SS3	Mr Jeremy Fisher	4	50-75	100-150	1/85-12/85
*SS4	Peter Rabbit	7	50-75	100-150	1/85-12/85
*SS11	Mrs Tiggy Winkle	5	50-75	100-150	1/85-12/85

SS26	Yock Yock (in the tub)	1⅞	50-75	100-150	1/86-6/86
SS27	Peter Rabbit (in the watering can)	3¼	50-75	100-150	1/86-6/86

YOUNG FRIENDS SERIES

SS5	'Puppy Love' (one dog washing another) black & brown, also black & white	4½	30-40	60-80	1/85-12/85
SS6	'I Spy' (two kittens in basket) available in tabby or white	4½	30-40	60-80	1/85-12/85
SS16	'Menu For Today' (puppy and kitten with cat food) brown & white or brown & tabby	3½	30-40	60-80	1/85-12/85
SS17	'Sharing' (dog & cat with bowl of milk)	3½	30-40	60-80	1/85-12/85

COUNTRYSIDE SERIES

SS8	'Contentment' (brown & white rabbit & young) also available in black & white	4¾	30-40	60-80	1/85-12/85
SS9	'Bright Eyes' (brown rabbit) also in black	4½	30-40	60-80	1/85-12/85
SS10	'Mind How You Go' (goose & goslings)	5¼	40-50	80-100	1/85-12/85
*SS13	'Happy Landing' (swan)	5	40-50	80-100	1/85-12/85
SS14	'The Chase' (3 dogs scrambling over a wall)	—	40-50	80-100	1/85-12/85
*SS15	'Hide and Seek' (3 dogs playing in a rock pool)	4½	40-50	80-100	1/85-12/85
SS18	'Planning Ahead' (squirrel with nuts)	3	20-30	40-60	1/85-12/85
SS19	'Early Bird' (wren)	2½	20-30	40-60	6/85-12/85
SS20	Golden Retriever	—	40-50	80-100	1/85-12/85
SS21	Pointer	—	40-50	80-100	6/85-12/85
SS22	English Setter	—	40-50	80-100	6/85-12/85
SS28	Robin	2¾	20-30	40-60	1/86-6/86
SS29	Blue Tit	2¾	20-30	40-60	1/86-6/86
SS30	Chaffinch	2¾	20-30	40-60	1/86-6/86

THELWELL SERIES

SS7	'I forgive you' (in grey or bay)	4	50-75	100-150	1/85-12/85
SS12	'Early Bath' (in grey or bay)	4¾	50-75	100-150	1/85-12/85

*on wood base

Beswick Bears

These superb resin models were produced under licence by the Royal Doulton Retail Division and marketed through Royal Doulton Shops, Lawleys and Factory Shops. Manufacturerd by an outside agency, they were packed in the standard green John Beswick box, with 'Beswick Bears' printed on the side. An additional gold sticker identified the particular model inside the box. The green baise base had a green adhesive label giving the model name and number together with a short rhyme.

The characters are all doing something different at a Teddy Bears picnic and the colours used on each model blend well and present a very natural group.

Available only during 1993 at very few outlets and at a very affordable price of £9.95, these models could easily become a very collectable series.

Each model is impressed with the Beswick 'B' mark.

Model No	Name of Model	Height inches	Current Value £	$	Production Period
BB001	William	2¼	15-20	30-40	1993 only
BB002	Billly	4	15-20	30-40	1993 only
BB003	Harry	3¼	15-20	30-40	1993 only
BB004	Bobby	4	15-20	30-40	1993 only
BB005	James	3¾	15-20	30-40	1993 only
BB006	Susie	3½	15-20	30-40	1993 only
BB007	Angela	3¼	15-20	30-40	1993 only
BB008	Charlotte	4	15-20	30-40	1993 only
BB009	Sam	3½	15-20	30-40	1993 only
BB010	Lizzy	2¼	15-20	30-40	1993 only
BB011	Emily	3½	15-20	30-40	1993 only
BB012	Sarah	3¼	15-20	30-40	1993 only

Country Cousins

Made of Resin, manufactured in (the country of) China and marketed by the Royal Doulton Retail Division, this series of 17 different small animals has a green baize base with a sticker describing the model and marked 'Beswick International'. Introduced in October 1994.

Model No	Name of Model	Current Value £	$
PM 2101	Sweet Suzie	4.99	RRP
PM 2102	Peter	5.50	RRP
PM 2103	Harry	6.50	RRP
PM 2104	Michael	5.50	RRP
PM 2105	Bertram	9.99	RRP
PM 2106	Leonardo	9.99	RRP
PM 2107	Lilly	8.99	RRP
PM 2108	Patrick	7.99	RRP
PM 2109	Jamie	8.99	RRP
PM 2110	Not used		
PM 2111	Mum and Lizzy	10.99	RRP
PM 2112	Molly and Timmy	10.99	RRP
PM 2113	Polly and Sarah	12.99	RRP
PM 2114	Ted and Bill	12.99	RRP
PM 2115	Jack and Daisy	11.99	RRP
PM 2116	Alison and Debbie	10.99	RRP
PM 2117	Not used		
PM 2118	Not used		
PM 2119	Robert and Rosie	10.99	RRP
PM 2120	Sammy	7.99	RRP

Wall Plaques and Masks

(All models carry a Beswick backstamp)

Between the wars there was a rather bizarre fashion for adorning the living room walls with pottery portraits of chic young ladies or colourful characters. The Beswick artists catered for this trend between 1934 and 1939 and in that time produced no less than twenty different models. Varying in size between three and twelve inches, these wall masks were described as novelties in the catalogues and were available in assorted colourways, including a matt white glaze finish, at between two and three shillings each (10p and 15p). The fashionable ladies and cute little girls seem to have been the most popular and the modeller, Miss Greaves, has portrayed them with the very latest accessories, jaunty berets or cloche hats.

Appealing to a different taste were the character masks featuring either a Jester, an Indian, a Patriotic Soldier or the favourite Dickens characters Tony Weller and MrMicawber. On the reverse of Mr Micawber, the eternal optimist, is his famous line "until something turns up, I have nothing to bestow but advice'.' The Dickens subjects were the speciality of Mr Watkin who later modelled the same personalities in the form of character jugs.

Human faces were not the only subjects considered suitable for wall plaques; Beswick also produced bas-relief galleons and yachts, baskets of flowers, butterflies and the famous flights of birds. So distinctive are they that they have been catalogued in a section of their own.

Model No	Name of Model	Height inches	Current Value £	$	Production Period
197	Girl with beret	6	150-200	300-400	1934-1954
263	Galleon	10	75-100	150-200	1934-1954
274	Tony Weller	7½	75-100	150-200	1934-1954
277	Lady with beret in profile	—	150-200	300-400	1934-1954
279	Jester	5¼	75-100	150-200	1934-1954
280	Mr Micawber	9	75-100	150-200	1934-1954
282	Indian	7½	75-100	150-200	1934-1954
314	Girl with curly hair & beret	9½	150-200	300-400	1934-1954
362	Girl with beret & scarf	—	150-200	300-400	1935-1954
363	Lady with beret & scarf in profile	—	150-200	300-400	1935-1954
364	Girl with beret & pom-pom	—	150-200	300-400	1935-1954
365	Girl with beret	—	150-200	300-400	1935-1954
366	Girl with hat	—	150-200	300-400	1935-1954
367	Lady with hat & scarf in profile	—	150-200	300-400	1935-1954
380	Girl with hat	9½	150-200	300-400	1936-1954
392	Child lying down	6¼	150-200	300-400	1936-1954
393	Girl with plait	8½	150-200	300-400	1936-1954
419	Floral wall hoop	12	60-80	120-175	1936-1954
420	Floral wall triangle	—	60-80	120-175	1936-1954
436	Lady with beads	12	200-250	400-500	1936-1954
449	Lady with hat & spotted scarf	12½	200-300	400-500	1936-1954
457	Genie	9¼	150-175	300-350	1936-1954
483	Girl – hands on head	9	150-200	300-400	1937-1954
507	The Gleaners	11	125-150	250-300	1937-1940
508	The Angelus	11	125-150	250-300	1937-1940
551	Basket of Flowers	10	100-125	200-250	1937-1954
556	Basket of Flowers	10½	100-125	200-250	1937-1954
557	Bowl of Flowers	6½	100-125	200-250	1937-1954
564	Bullrushes	14	100-125	200-250	1937-1940
565	Bowl of Flowers	5½	100-125	200-250	1937-1954
571	Bowl of Flowers	—	100-125	200-250	1937-1954
612	Boy with red hair	7¼	200-250	400-500	1938-1954
614	Butterfly	—	60-80	120-175	1938-1954
710	Lovers	8	100-125	200-250	1939-1940
714	Three Cherubs 'Hear No Evil' Etc	6 x 4½	100-150	200-300	1939-1940
715	'A World Without Friends Would Be Like A Garden Without Flowers'	9½ x 7½	150-175	300-350	1939-1940
719	'One of the Best'	9½ x 7½	150-175	300-350	1939-1940
723	'Those Who Bring Sunshine To The Lives Of Others Cannot Keep It From Themselves'	9½ x 7½	150-175	300-350	1939-1940
724	'Don't Worry It May Never Happen'	8 x 8¾	150-175	300-350	1939-1940

739	'Life's a Melody If You'll Only Hum the Tune'	8 x 8¾	150-175	300-350	1939-1940
740	'When You Are Up to Your Neck in Hot Water Think of the Kettle and Sing'	8 x 8¾	150-175	300-350	1939-1940
741	Lovers	8	100-125	200-250	1939-1945
837	Plain Plaque	16 dia	50-75	100-150	1940-1954
842	Gargoyle Mask	4½ x 5½	75-100	150-200	1940-1954
1632	Yacht No. 2242	7¾	75-100	150-200	1959-1962
*2233	Cat and Dog	9 x 6¼	50-75	100-150	1969-1970
*2235	Basset Hound	9 x 6¼	50-75	100-150	1969-1970
*2236	Cat	9 x 6¼	50-75	100-150	1969-1970
*2268	Poodle	6 x 4¾	50-75	100-150	1969-1970

Concave models in white matt finish

2699 *to* **2702** *The four horse head plaques taken from the respective horse models. (see listing on page 45)*

Part Three: Decorative Wares

(All models carry a Beswick backstamp, except 1988 re-introductions for Whyte & Mackay. Since 1988 they are marked Royal Doulton)

Advertising Ware

China and earthenware are ideal advertising media. They are durable, easy to clean and before the advent of plastic, they dominated the shop shelves.

Even today, although they are usually more expensive to produce than plastic they are still the chosen promotional tools for many breweries and distillers, who argue that a finely modelled ceramic decanter is less likely to be thrown away than a plain glass bottle and so their advertisement is more enduring. For over twenty years Beswick have been responsible for the figurative whisky containers, many in the form of animals, for Peter Thomson of Perth and most of these are still being made today. Beswick revived their association with Bass by re-issuing the Lord Mayor jug (first produced in 1961) for a short period in 1987.

Double Diamond was the first beer to be promoted by Beswick and the brewer's well-known city gent character was modelled as a teapot in 1958, followed by a jug and a wall-plaque in 1960. Other familiar pub artifacts of this period include the Babycham fawn and the Courage cockerel. However, Beswick did not only cater for the spirit trade, their first recorded advertising piece was for Heatmaster who made teapots encased in thermal jackets. For this firm they made a liqueur set with the decanter in the form of a friar. It is not known what connection was intended between the liqueur container and Heatmaster's products, other than that they are all warming!

One of the most unusual advertising pieces in the collection features a little cobbler stitching a shoe which was made to celebrate Timpson's centenary in 1965.

Model No	Name of Model	Height inches	Current Value £	$	Production Period
1201	Friar Liqueur Set comprising tray & six measures for Heatmaster	8¼	60-80	120-175	1950-1954
1517	Double Diamond man container	8	100-150	200-300	1958-1965
1544	Barrel Lamp with tap	—	30-40	60-80	1958-1965
1587	Small Barrel (Sherry)	4¼	30-40	60-80	1959-1965
1598	Large Barrel (Port or Whisky)	5	30-40	60-80	1959-1965
1615	Babycham Fawn	4	30-40	60-80	1959-1974
1625	Woodbine ash tray	—	20-25	40-50	1959-1960
1672	Double Diamond face jug	6½	100-150	200-300	1960-1961
1679	Double Diamond Public House Plaque	8¾ x 10W	125-150	250-300	1960-1965

No.	Description	Size			Years
1680	Double Diamond man Plaque	5¼ x 5¼	75-100	150-200	1960-1965
1681	Double Diamond dog Plaque	4¾ L x 1¾	60-80	120-175	1960-1965
1741/1	Lord Mayor water jug (red bottle top)	8½	50-60	100-120	1961-1967
1741/2	Lord Mayor water jug (green bottle top)	8½	40-50	80-100	1986-1987
1820	Barrel B	2⅛	5-10	10-20	1962-1986
1821	Carrera's 'Guardsman' Cigarettes Tankard	5¼	30-40	60-80	1962-1965
1829	Catto's Sportsman figure and dog	11½	150-200	300-400	1962-1965
1850	Double Diamond lamp	6⅛	30-35	60-70	1962-1965
1856	Double Diamond dish	—	15-20	30-40	1962-1965
1869	Dubonnet stand	7½ x 4¼	20-25	40-50	1963-1967
1870	Dubonnet bottle	5½	20-25	40-50	1963-1967
1871	Dubonnet poodle	4⅛	60-80	120-160	1963-1967
1872	Dubonnet bulldog	3¾	60-80	120-160	1963-1967
1946	Timpsons the shoemaker dish	3½	40-50	80-100	1964-1966
1955	Smiths Crisps Plaque	7¼ x 2	35-45	70-115	1964-1965
1983	Canada Dry ash tray	9	20-25	40-50	1964-1967
1984	Rothmans lamp	4½	30-35	60-70	1964-1967
1990	Dulux dog	12½	225-275	450-600	1964-1970
1999	Bath oil bottle & stopper for Cussons	7½	10-15	20-30	1966-1967
2000	Covered bath salt jar for Cussons	5¼	10-15	20-30	1966-1967
2001	Bourne & Hollingsworth ash tray	8 x 6½	20-25	40-50	1964-1967
2009	Skol lamp	6	30-35	60-70	1965-1968
2010	Double Diamond lamp	5½	30-35	60-70	1965-1968
2011	Skol lamp	6	30-35	60-70	1965-1968
2018	Double Diamond lamp	5½	30-35	60-70	1965-1968
2033	Fishermans flask B	3¾	10-15	20-30	1965-1970
2047	Gallagher ash bowl	9x 7	20-25	40-50	1965-1968
2048	Les Leston steering wheel ash bowl	7 ¼	30-40	60-80	1965-1967
*2051	Nessie (Loch Ness Monster) B, 2 models: one with head stopper one with base stopper	3	5-10	10-25	1965-1986
2052	Piccadilly ash tray	8⅛	20-25	40-50	1965-1970
2053	Gallagher water jug	5⅜	25-30	50-60	1965-1970
2055	Craven A oval ash tray	11 x 6⅝	20-25	40-50	1966-1970
2056	Pheasant flask B	3½	10-15	20-30	1966-1970
2057	Pike flask B	3½	10-15	20-30	1966-1970
2058	Deer flask B	3½	10-15	20-30	1966-1970
2060	Hunts (lady rider on horse jumping fence) Plaque	7⅜	150-175	300-350	1966-1970
2076	Robert Burns cottage flask B	3½	10-15	20-30	1966-1971
2077	Edinburgh Castle flask B	3½	10-15	20-30	1966-1970
2079	Watneys Plaque	6¼	35-45	70-100	1966-1970
2086	Beswick Plaque (Black & Gold)	2½	20-25	40-50	1966-1980
2088	Peters Griffin Woodward bust USA dept. store	3½	50-60	100-125	1967-1970
2092	Peters Griffin Woodward character jug USA dept. store	5	60-80	120-160	1967-1970
*2104	Eagle flask B	4⅜	5-10	10-20	1967-1986
2115	Pall Mall ash tray	9¾ x 4¾	20-25	40-50	1967-1969
2180	Tower Bridge flask	3½	10-15	20-30	1968-1971

2185	Arundel Castle flask	$4\frac{1}{2}$	10-15	20-30	1968-1971
2192	Benson & Hedges square ash tray	5	20-25	40-50	1968-1975
2206	Deer flask	$3\frac{1}{2}$	10-15	20-30	1968-1975
2207	Trout flask	$3\frac{1}{2}$	10-15	20-30	1968-1975
2208	Pheasant flask	$3\frac{1}{2}$	10-15	20-30	1968-1975
2218	Benson & Hedges orb ash tray	7 D	20-25	40-50	1968-1975
2219	Craven A ash tray	8 D	20-25	40-50	1968-1970
2237	Babycham concave Plaque	$6\frac{1}{4} \times 3\frac{3}{8}$	50-75	100-150	1968-1970
2241	Hamlet ash tray	$7\frac{1}{2} \times 5$	20-25	40-50	1968-1975
2260	Bemax jar & lid	—	25-30	40-50	1969-1970
2261	Hamlet cigars ash tray	$6\frac{1}{8} \times 6$	20-25	40-50	1969-1975
2280	Chante Clair cockerel jug	$9\frac{3}{4}$	100-150	200-300	1969-1971
2281	Golden Eagle flask B	$10\frac{7}{8}$	45-60	90-125	1969-1984
2318	Golf Ball flask B	$1\frac{5}{8}$ D	10-15	20-30	1970-1986
2349	Robert Burns flask B	—	50-75	100-175	1970-1975
**2350	Haggis flask B	$2\frac{1}{2}$	5-10	10-20	1971-1986
2486	Bass Charrington (young couple behind letter E)	9	75-100	150-200	1973-1976
2487	Bass Charrington (rugby players behind letter E)	9	75-100	150-200	1973-1976
2488	Bass Charrington (squire & friend behind letter E)	9	75-100	150-200	1973-1976
2506	Bass Charington (Minton ewer jug)	$6\frac{3}{4}$	30-40	60-80	1974-1976
2514	White Horse whisky (horse)	$6\frac{3}{4}$	200-250	400-500	1974-1976
***2518	Worthington (butcher & baker behind letter E)	9	100-125	200-250	1974-1975
***2519	Worthington (woman & dog behind letter E)	9	100-125	200-250	1974-1975
***2520	Worthington (parson & policeman behind letter E)	9	100-125	200-250	1974-1975
2561	Grouse for Mathew Gloag Ltd	$9\frac{3}{8}$	75-85	150-200	1976-1984
*2583	Osprey flask B	$7\frac{3}{4}$	40-60	80-120	1977-1986
**2636	Squirrel flask B	$3\frac{1}{2}$	10-15	20-30	1978-1986
*2639	Kestrel flask B	$6\frac{1}{2}$	40-60	80-120	1979-1986
*2640	Buzzard flask B	$6\frac{1}{2}$	40-60	80-120	1979-1986
*2641	Merlin flask B	$6\frac{1}{2}$	40-60	80-120	1979-1986
*2642	Peregrine flask B	$6\frac{1}{2}$	40-60	80-120	1979-1986
2670	Bunratty castle (5000 edition)	6	30-40	60-80	1980-1983
*2678	Golden Eagle flask B	$10\frac{1}{2}$	50-60	100-120	1984-1987
**2686	Otter flask B	$2\frac{1}{4}$	10-15	20-30	1981-1986
**2687	Badger flask B	3	10-15	20-30	1981-1986
**2693	Seal flask B	$3\frac{7}{8}$	10-15	20-30	1981-1986
*2781	Tawny Owl flask B	$6\frac{1}{4}$	40-60	80-125	1986-1987
*2809	Barn Owl flask B	$6\frac{3}{4}$	40-60	80-125	1986-1987
*2825	Short Eared Owl flask B	$6\frac{1}{2}$	40-60	80-125	1986-1987
2826/1	Snowy Owl flask B	$\frac{3}{4}$	50-70	100-150	1986-1987
*2826/2	Snowy Owl flask W&M	$6\frac{1}{2}$	40-60	80-125	1986-1986

B = Beneagles whisky container for Peter Thomson (Perth) Ltd.
D= diameter
*Re-introduced 1987 for Whyte & Mackay(Glasgow), now current and carrying the Royal Doulton backstamp
** Re-introduced 1987-1991 for Whyte & Mackay
***Limited production

Christmas Around the World

(All carry the Beswick mark)

There are a growing number of collectors who seem to enjoy Christmas all year long by tracking down pieces with colourful, seasonal imagery. The fashion for collecting plates with a Christmas theme developed in the USA and it was originally for an American audience that Beswick introduced a series of annual plates depicting 'Christmas Around the World'. In order to convey the distinctive traditions of festivities in other lands, several different artists were invited to contribute to this collection and their artwork was then modelled in low relief by Beswick artists. Harry Sales, the company's design manager, visualised the first, 'Old England' in 1972. Chavela Castrejon was commissioned to design 'Christmas in Mexico' issued in 1973 and Dimitri Yordanov was responsible for 'Christmas in Bulgaria' for the 1974 plate. The remaining four plates were all designed by Alton Toby, his final scene of 'Christmas in America' completing the set of seven in 1978.

In addition to these plates, the Beswick artists experimented with a few relief modelled rectangular plaques portraying yuletide scenes in Dickensian mood but it would appear these did not go into production in any great quantity.

Plates & Plaques

Model No	Description	Size inches	Current Value £	$	Plate or Plaque	Issue Date
2376	Christmas 1972	11¼ x 5½	200-250	400-500	Plaque	1972
2393	Christmas in England	8 x 8	30-40	60-80	Plate	1972
2419	Christmas in Mexico	8 x 8	30-40	60-80	Plate	1973
2430	Christmas 1973	11¼ x 5½	200-250	400-500	Plaque	1973
2443	Regent Street	11 x 7	125-150	250-300	Plaque	1973
2444	Christmas Ornament		75-100	150-200	Plaque	1973
2462	Christmas in Bulgaria	8 x 8	30-40	60-80	Plate	1974
2522	Christmas in Norway	8 x 8	30-40	60-80	Plate	1975
2538	Christmas in Holland	8 x 8	30-40	60-80	Plate	1976
2567	Christmas in Poland	8 x 8	30-40	60-80	Plate	1977
2598	Christmas in America	8 x 8	30-40	60-85	Plate	1978

Christmas Carol Tankards

(All carry the Beswick Mark)

Dickens also provided the inspiration for the limited edition collection of tankards launched in 1971. Each year a scene from his classic *A Christmas Carol* was vividly modelled in low relief and admirably captured the spirit of the traditional English yuletide. The set of twelve was completed in 1982 and although the edition size was published as 15,000 each year, it is believed that the final number produced was less than this, with most going to the United States, Canada and Australia. However, the British collector can still find them at antique fairs and markets.

Model No	Description	Value £	$	Issue Date
2351	Cratchit & Scrooge	40-50	80-100	1971
2375	Carolers	40-50	80-100	1972
2423	Solicitation	40-50	80-100	1973
2445	Marley's Ghost	30-40	60-80	1974
2523	Ghost of Christmas Past	30-40	60-80	1975
2539	Ghost of Christmas Present	30-40	60-80	1976
2568	Ghost of Christmas Present	30-40	60-80	1977
2599	Ghost of Christmas Present	30-40	60-80	1978
2624	Ghost of Christmas Future	30-40	60-80	1979
2657	Scrooge Visits His Own Grave	30-40	60-80	1980
2692	Scrooge Going to Church	30-40	60-80	1981
2764	Christmas at Bob Cratchit's	40-50	80-100	1982

The final annual Christmas Tankard in the series of 12 was 1982 and this is the hardest to find

Commemoratives

(All carry the Beswick mark)

Royal Commemoratives produced by Beswick form a small but interesting collection. Like other pottery companies Beswick issued pieces to commemorate the coronation of HRH Edward VIII but when he suddenly abdicated on December 10 1936, new wares featuring HRH George VI had to be prepared.

   As well as two mugs, of which one was musical, Beswick obtained the reproduction rights for a collection of souvenirs modelled by Felix Weiss. These unusual commemoratives all depicted the bust of George VI and are listed below.

   The next Royal coronation was that of HRH Elizabeth II in 1953 and the selection of mugs and trays issued for this occasion are also detailed below.

Model No	Name of Model	Current Value £	$	Production Period
377	Edward VIII Plaque	60-80	120-160	1936-1937
445	Edward VIII Coronation tankard	30-40	60-80	1936-1937
446	Edward VIII Coronation mug	15-20	30-40	1936-1937
451	Edward VIII bust	60-80	120-160	1936-1937
458	Edward VIII covered jar	60-80	120-160	1936-1937
461	George VI Coronation musical mug	75-100	150-200	1937-1938
462	George VI Coronation mug	15-20	30-40	1937-1938
468	George VI bust	60-80	120-160	1937-1938
469	George VI bust	50-60	100-120	1937-1938
470	George VI plaque	60-80	120-160	1937-1938
471	George VI plaque	50-60	100-120	1937-1938
472	George VI bookend	50-60	100-120	1937-1938
1250	Elizabeth II Coronation mug	15-20	30-40	1952-1954
1251	Elizabeth II Coronation beaker	15-20	30-40	1952-1954
1252	Elizabeth II Embossed Coronation mug	20-25	40-50	1952-1954
1253	Elizabeth II Coronation tray (large)	20-25	40-50	1952-1954
1254	Elizabeth II Coronation tray (small)	15-20	30-40	1952-1954

Shakespeare Series Ware

(All carry the Beswick mark)

The plays of William Shakespeare (1564-1616) have been a fertile source of inspiration for Beswick artists. Mr Hallam, Mr Gredington and Mr Orwell have interpreted some of the most famous scenes in a series of jugs, tankards and mugs, superbly modelled in low relief. *Romeo and Juliet*, Shakespeare's first tragedy and perhaps his best known work, is represented by a jug and a wall plaque both depicting the fond farewell. The other plaque in the series features characters from the famous comedy *As You Like It* and the quotation "That would I, were I of all kingdoms king". Suitable inscriptions appear on all the Shakespeare wares. Hamlet's famous soliloquy "To be or not to be" is inscribed on a tankard depicting a scene from the play and a jug features the Prince of Denmark with his father's ghost and the quotation "Hamlet — be thou a spirit of health?" Sir John Falstaff, Shakespeare's jovial knight also features on both a jug and a tankard. He was so popular with audiences in the sixteenth century that he appears in *Henry IV* Part I, *Henry V* and later in *The Merry Wives of Windsor*.

All these Shakespearean wares so far discussed are relatively easy to find today but the last two depicting scenes from *A Midsummer Night's Dream* which were added to the set in 1955, can be quite elusive.

Model No	Name of Model	Height inches	Current Value £	$	Production Period
1126	Falstaff jug	8	60-80	120-160	1948-1973
1127	Falstaff tankard	4	25-30	50-80	1948-1973
1146	Hamlet jug	8¼	60-80	120-160	1949-1973
1147	Hamlet tankard	4¼	25-30	50-60	1949-1973
1209	As You Like It wall plaque	12 dia	80-100	160-200	1950-1969
1210	Romeo & Juliet wall plaque	12 dia	80-100	160-200	1951-1969
1214	Juliet jug	8¼	60-80	120-160	1951-1973
1215	Juliet mug	4	25-30	50-60	1951-1973
1366	A Midsummer Night's Dream – jug	8	75-100	150-200	1955-1973
1368	A Midsummer Night's Dream – mug	4¼	40-60	80-120	1955-1973
2213	Bust of Shakespeare	3	30-40	60-80	1968-1970
2243	Bust of Shakespeare on pedestal	5	40-50	80-100	1968-1970

Trentham Art Wares

During the 1930s a seven year agreement was made between Beswick and Hardy, a wholesaler based in Nottingham, for items to be designed and produced at Beswick, but to be marketed under the name of 'Trentham Art Wares'.

Approximately two hundred different items were produced and marked with the Beswick model number and 'Made in England' impressed on the base together with the 'Trentham Art Wares' backstamp. Most pieces were vases or jugs but there were approximately thirty animals, figures or birds and it is likely that these only carried the backstamp.

The agreement lapsed in 1941 and Beswick were then free to continue production of the more popular items, but carrying only their own backstamp or impressed mark.

Several of these pieces continued in production until the mid sixties and the following list gives all known model numbers which were subject to this agreement.

Model Numbers

21-48	380/84/85	653-657	902-914
76/77	422/24/28	668	918-922
79-81	431/32/34/35	675-680	955-959
91/94/95/98	439/40	688	987
129-132	444	693/94/99	
136	447-449	700/02	
140	490/92/94/95/96	731	
148-167	498-500	760-62/65	
289-292	503-505	770-784	
299-301	546-548	800-809	
306/07	550/52/54/55	813/15/19	
345-357	558/60/62/63	827/29	
362-367	566/68-70	836/38	
373/79	573		

Britannia Collection

(All backstamped Beswick)

This range of ceramic studies is taken from the existing Beswick collection, with the exception of the Special Commission Unicorn, and is finished in a rich bronze glaze with subtle shading. This new decorative process was developed by Graham Tongue, Design Manager of the John Beswick Studio.

Model No	Name of Model	Height inches	Value £	$	Production Period
868	Huntsman	10	70-90	140-190	1989-1992
*981	Stag (small)	9	20-25	40-50	1989-1992
1018	Bald Eagle	7¼	30-40	60-80	1989-1992
*2542	Hereford Bull	7½	100-125	200-250	1989-1992
*2549	Polled Hereford Bull	6¼	40-50	80-100	1989-1992
2629	Stag (large)	13½	100-125	200-250	1989-1992
*2688	Spirit of the Wind (horse)	9	40-50	80-100	1989-1992
2760	Pheasant	10½	100-125	200-250	1989-1992
*2914	Spirit of Earth (shire horse)	8½	40-50	80-100	1989-1992
*2986	Setter	8½	40-50	80-100	1989-1992
*3011	Pointer	8⅜	40-50	80-100	1989-1992
*3021	Unicorn	9	50-60	100-120	1989-1992
*3066	Retriever	7½	40-50	80-100	1989-1992

*on ceramic base

Catalogue Specials

Since 1987 a number of current items have been mounted on ceramic bases, for direct purchase from mail order catalogues.

Most had a polished brass name-plate affixed to the base, with a suitably descriptive title. Now discontinued, they are an unusual addition to the Beswick collection, but do tend to take up a lot of space.

In addition, there was at least one example of a Shire horse (2914) being mounted on a ceramic base with a green top instead of the production 'earth' colour.

This order was for an American TV station and all were sold in this way. The backstamp was circular and read 'Beswick — Made in England'.

Other combinations can also be found.

Model No	Name-plate Title	Model names
1558/1678	'Watch It'	Siamese Cat/Mouse
2950/1436	'Good Friends'	Playful puppy 'Nap Time'/Kitten
1460/1436	'Sharing'	Dachshund sitting/Kitten
818/1034	'Horses Great & Small'	Shire/Shetland Foal
2267/2110	'Jenny's Baby'	Donkey/Donkey Foal
1765/1828	'Ewe and I'	Sheep
999/1000	—	Doe and Fawn
1452/1453	—	Pigs
1362/1249	—	Cow and Calf — black
1362/1249	—	Cow and Calf — brown
1886/3093	'Playtime'	Kitten/Ball of Wool
1501/2262/63	'Tally Ho!'	Huntsman and 2 Hounds
2689/2536	—	Black Beauty and Foal (in gloss)

Models mounted on a wood plinth

New introductions for 1994 included the following current models mounted on a wooden base with a brass plaque. All are gloss finish.

Model No.	Model name	Current Value £	$	Production Period
3075/1827	Charolais Cow and Calf	47.00	RRP	1993-C
1362/1249	Freisan Cow and Calf	47.00	RRP	1993-C
1360/1827	Hereford Cow and Calf	47.00	RRP	1993-C
1345/1249	Jersey Cow and Calf	47.00	RRP	1993-C
1765/1828	Black Faced Sheep and Lamb	24.95	RRP	1993-C
1452	Sow — Large White	17.95	RRP	1993-C
1453	Boar — Large White	19.95	RRP	1993-C
1016	Standing Fox	24.95	RRP	1993-C
999/1000	Doe and Fawn	35.00	RRP	1993-C

Backstamps

The dating of backstamps holds a great deal of interest for all collectors and the task has not been made easy by the fairly wide variety used by Beswick. In addition, several designs of adhesive labels have been used since the late 1950s up until 1989, when the practice ceased. In the late 1960s, horses and cattle had their name printed on a label, which was tied around the neck. This practice ceased about 1972. Round about 1987 the tie-on label method was revived on most items produced at that time, but this was a standard green John Beswick type and did not apply specifically to that model. These are still in use today. Other specially designed tie-on labels have recently been used on the Little Loveables, English Country Friend and Pig Prom series.

Left: impressed name and number. Base large enough to accommodate both. In use 1938-1972. Right: Impressed number only on smaller base. Backstamped name. In use 1938-72

Small flat base with the backstamp "England" only. In use 1945-1972

***Thunderbirds** special stamp. In use 1992 only.*

Backstamp used on base for specially commissioned animal series. In use 1990-1992 only

*Left: Special backstamp for large size Jemima Puddleduck. Produced for Beswick Centenary, 1994 only. Right: Backstamp used for **Little Loveable** Clowns. 1992-1994 only.*

Transfer backstamp in use 1985-1990

Special backstamp for Colin Melbourne models between 1957-1970

Backstamp occasionally used during the 1980s

Left: Backstamp mix of transfer and handwritten marks. All gold in colour. In use 1948-1967. Right: Transfer backstamp. All Gold in colour, 1949-1967

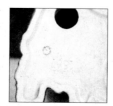

*Popular mark, used on selected ranges only from about 1963 until 1971. The mark has "Made in England" when used on some **Connoisseur** models. The 1963-1971 mark has again been used on the more recent **Little Loveables, & English Country Friends** series*

This mark seems to have been widely used from the early 1950s and included the Beatrix Potter, Walt Disney, David Hand and Snow White series together with a wide range of animal and bird models. A large number of decorative pieces also had this mark. It seems to have continued in use until about 1965

This mark can be found on almost any piece of Beswick dating from the mid to late 1950s up to the present day

Special backstamps for "Hummel" figures. Model number sometimes impressed. In use 1940-1947

This is an impressed mark and was in use from about 1954 until 1971

Beswick Stick-on Labels

From the early 1960s, several designs of stick-on label were used and applied to most pieces leaving the factory.

Used for a short period in the late 1960s

Used extensively on Ornamental Ware from the mid-1950s to mid 1960s

Used extensively on all animal models from about 1960-1970

Used on smaller animals and birds from about 1970 until 1989

*Backstamp widely used from about 1935 until 1971. It is a mark intended to convey the importance of **Ware** as against **Novelties** and was only used on decorative pieces (vases etc). Most novelties (anything except vases) had too small a base area to accommodate this stamp and other, smaller stamps were used.*

Trentham Art Ware. Used for all Ornamental Ware produced for Hardy, a Nottingham based wholesaler

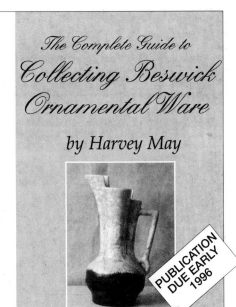

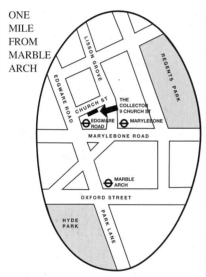

WE ARE COMING
from UK International Ceramics Ltd

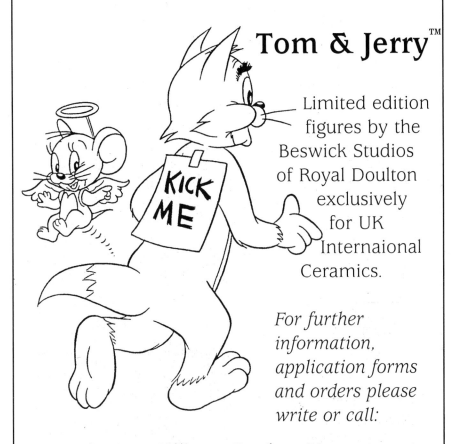

Tom & Jerry™

Limited edition figures by the Beswick Studios of Royal Doulton exclusively for UK Internaional Ceramics.

For further information, application forms and orders please write or call:

Miss Zoe Gilligan, Product Manager,
UK International Ceramics,
10 Wilford Bridge Spur,
Melton, Woodbridge, Suffolk
IP12 1RJ, England
Tel: 01394 386662   Fax: 01394 386742

Limited Editions

NOTES